REFLE
OF LONELINESS

HEROINES?

Certain fictional women have become part of western mythology. They are the stars of novels, films, radio and TV programmes, which have caught the imagination of generations of women. What is the secret of their magnetism?

This new feminist series about literary heroines investigates their lasting appeal. Each writer explores her chosen heroine's relationships with other characters in the novel, with her own author, with readers past and present, and lastly with herself. These characters all touch chords of reality for us. By their very 'ordinariness' they demonstrate that, in the most general feminist sense, all women are heroines.

For general readers as well as students, these concise, elegantly-written books will delight all lovers – and even haters – of the original classics.

Titles in the series include:

Mary Evans *Reflecting on Anna Karenina*

Pat Macpherson *Reflecting on Jane Eyre*

Rebecca O'Rourke *Reflecting on the Well of Loneliness*

REBECCA O'ROURKE

REFLECTING ON THE WELL OF LONELINESS

ROUTLEDGE
London and New York

First published in 1989
by Routledge
11 New Fetter Lane, London EC4P 4EE

Simultaneously published in the USA and Canada
by Routledge
a division of Routledge, Chapman and Hall Inc.
29 West 35th Street, New York, NY 10001

© 1989 Rebecca O'Rourke

Typeset by Witwell Ltd, Southport
**Printed in Great Britain
by Cox & Wyman Ltd, Reading**

All rights reserved. No part of this book may be
reprinted or reproduced or utilized in any form or
by any electronic, mechanical, or other means, now
known or hereafter invented, including photocopying
and recording, or in any information storage or
retrieval system, without permission in writing from
the publishers.

British Library Cataloguing in Publication Data

O'Rourke, Rebecca, *1955-* .
Reflecting on The Well of Loneliness
— (Heroines?)
1. Fiction in English. Hall, Radclyffe,
1886–1943
I. Title   II. Series
823′.912

ISBN 0–415–01841–2

Library of Congress Cataloging in Publication Data

O'Rourke, Rebecca.
Reflecting on The Well of Loneliness/
by Rebecca O'Rourke.
p.   cm. — (Heroines?)
Bibliography: p.
Includes index.
1. Hall, Radclyffe.   Well of loneliness.
2. Lesbianism in literature.   3. Social isolation
in literature.   4. Heroines in literature.
I. Title.   II. Series.

| PR6015.A33W56 | 1989 | 89–6211 |
| 823′.912—dc20 | | CIP |

ISBN 0–415–01841–2

CONTENTS

Acknowledgements	vii
Preface	ix
Chapter One: Who is Stephen Gordon, What is She?	1
Chapter Two: Stephen Gordon and Other People in her Life	8
Chapter Three: How does Stephen Gordon get on with Other Women?	40
Chapter Four: How does the Reader get on with Stephen Gordon?	90
Chapter Five: Who reads *The Well of Loneliness*?	114
Conclusion	143
Bibliography	145

FOR RUTH, AND ALL OUR FUTURES

ACKNOWLEDGEMENTS

WRITING THIS BOOK entails a debt to all who lived with my enthusiasm for it and, perhaps more importantly, those who sustained me through times of personal upheaval when I had neither the confidence nor interest to continue work on it. In this respect, Gill Davies, whose idea the series was, Mary Evans, and Elizabeth Wilson have my especial thanks.

As well as personal friends, particularly Ruth and Jean, I owe an enormous debt to the women who assisted with and took part in the readership survey. The majority did not wish to be acknowledged by name and so I identified the responses on the basis of when *The Well of Loneliness* had been read. So, thank you to them and to: Anna, Avril, Caroline, Celia, Elizabeth, Gaby, Gwyneth, Harriet, Jackie, Jane, Jean, Jean, Jeanne, Joan, Julie, Katrin, Karen, Laura, Liz, Marty, Pam, Sandra, Sigrid, and Susannah.

PREFACE

THE WELL OF LONELINESS, Radclyffe Hall's fourth novel, was first published in 1928. It is the only one of her novels with an explicit lesbian theme, although she herself lived openly as a lesbian throughout her life.

It concerns Stephen Gordon, named for the son her parents wanted and never had. She is born into privilege, though as a child is often lonely. Almost from birth her father, Sir Philip, usurps the role of her mother (Lady Anna). Stephen is given a boy's name and directed towards such activities as riding, more usually associated with sons than with daughters. She is educated at home by two governesses, Mlle Duphot and Puddle, both of whom she remains in contact with throughout her life. Puddle and she make a home together for many years. As Stephen grows up, her estrangement from femininity becomes pronounced and this causes her a great deal of misery, not least because of the conflict it generates between her parents.

A violent outburst of temper follows Stephen's discovery of Collins, a domestic servant on whom she has a crush, in the arms of a footman. Following this, her father takes complete control of Stephen's upbringing and the novel hints heavily as to his reasons. Stephen is not like other girls and Sir Philip, who does not take his wife into his confidence, tells her never to expect that she will marry. Later, the friendship between Stephen and Martin Hallam appears to undermine this gloomy foreboding but Stephen is appalled by Martin's proposal of marriage when it finally comes and the latter quickly returns to

ix

Preface

the colonies. Shortly afterwards, Sir Philip meets with a fatal accident.

In the wake of this bereavement, Stephen becomes emotionally involved with Angela Crossby, the wife of a *nouveau riche* neighbour. In the scandal that follows, Lady Anna refuses to live in the same house as Stephen, effectively banishing her from Morton, the family home. Puddle and Stephen set up home in London where Stephen dedicates herself to writing, initially with some success. During a period of depression, which affects her writing, a friend, Brockett, urges her to go to Paris. Puddle has reservations about the lesbian society she is introduced to there, although she does not express them, and Stephen takes a house in Paris.

The outbreak of the First World War sends them back to England, although Stephen eventually joins an ambulance corps serving at the front. It is there she meets Mary Llewellyn, an orphan, who is to become her lover. The relationship proceeds slowly, with Mary taking the initiatives. After the war, they set up home together in Paris. The relationship comes under a good deal of stress: Lady Anna does not acknowledge it; Stephen experiences conflict between time for her writing and time for Mary: Mary soon becomes bored, having no occupation other than her life with Stephen. A friendship with Lady Massey and her daughter seems to offer respite, but it ends abruptly when the true nature of Stephen and Mary's relationship is learnt.

At this point, Stephen and Mary throw themselves into Parisian lesbian life, something experienced and presented, with ambivalence. Quite by chance, Martin Hallam comes back into their lives. He offers friendship to both initially but as his feelings for Mary gradually turn from affection to love, he and Stephen enter into a bitter contest. Stephen retains Mary's love and loyalty, but then sacrifices them. Mary is led to think Stephen is having an affair with another woman. Distraught, she rushes from the house, into Martin's arms. Stephen has arranged for him to be there.

Chapter One

WHO IS STEPHEN GORDON, WHAT IS SHE?

STEPHEN GORDON is the perfect hero. She is noble, accomplished, wealthy, self-sacrificing, honourable. She has only one flaw – that she is a woman. Women are never heroes. To be a heroine, the dictionary explains, is simply to be a woman with the qualities of a hero. To be a heroine in life and fiction is something entirely different. And its first condition is to be a woman, something far from straightforward for Stephen Gordon.

Before we look in detail at Stephen Gordon, at the tensions between heroes and heroines, between men and women, and between lesbianism and heterosexuality, it is important to establish what she is not. She is not Radclyffe Hall. Stating the obvious I may be, but the two are often conflated. *The Well of Loneliness* was Radclyffe Hall's fourth novel, written in 1927 when she was in her late forties. It is her only novel that takes lesbianism as its focus. In *The Life and Death of Radclyffe Hall* (1961), Lady Una Troubridge, writes that the decision to tackle the theme of lesbianism was long-standing. She was consulted about it, Radclyffe Hall realizing that however secure her literary reputation might be, a book that pleaded for tolerance towards homosexuality carried with it risks of public condemnation. Their experiences with the Psychical Research Society had made them less naïve in that respect. Other biographical writing confirms that Radclyffe Hall's intentions were to write an informative book 'accessible to the general public' (Troubridge, 1961: 81), that would set the record straight about sexual inversion.

Who is Stephen Gordon, What is She?

There is a link between Hall's own lesbianism and her desire to plead the case for public tolerance but *The Well of Loneliness* cannot be read as autobiography. The most significant change from fact to fiction is that Hall enjoyed the recognition and satisfaction of her sexuality with a number of women lovers. Nothing could be further from Hall's actual experience than the tortured self-denial that characterizes Stephen Gordon.

Radclyffe Hall's life offers a much more positive and optimistic account of lesbian existence than does her fiction. This was, I suspect, deliberate. Her cause could plead better from an appeal based on the suffering of homosexuals rather than from an account of their pleasures. That the book was tried under the obscenity laws is a most graphic indictment of the need for the tolerance and understanding that it argues for. The heroism of Hall, as persecuted author, becomes identified with that of the character of Stephen Gordon; each standing defiantly alone against a hostile, uncomprehending world. But, without denying Hall's courage, it has to be said that it wasn't like that. Unlike Stephen Gordon, who exists in a state of isolation for most of the novel, Radclyffe Hall had support both from a partner and the public.

The publicity surrounding its publication has ensured that *The Well of Loneliness* remains widely known, probably the only lesbian novel known as such by readers who are not lesbians. The classic novel of lesbian love, as the Corgi paperback (1968) puts it. In this context, it is important to know what it says about lesbianism and lesbian identity. It was written for a presumed heterosexual audience. What does this do to Stephen Gordon? Whose heroine does it make her? For heterosexual readers, there cannot be the usual process of identification and attachment. Stephen Gordon will not illuminate aspects of themselves for them: her role is to represent difference and otherliness. For lesbians there is more potential for identification but, as Chapter 5 will explore, Stephen Gordon is an uncomfortable and awkward model. She fixes lesbianism as a singular and clearly defined condition. Hall took sexologists' studies of lesbianism, particularly those

Who is Stephen Gordon, What is She?

of Havelock Ellis, and provided a fictional account of its pathology.

The book that Sir Philip consults in his library and which Stephen herself finds after his death is probably *Psychopathia Sexualis* by Dr R. von Krafft-Ebbing (1892). It gives few examples of female case-studies and almost all feature the criminally insane. It is likely that Case 31 served as a model for Stephen Gordon. It is the only female treated at length and echoes Stephen Gordon at many points, especially in her pleas: 'Gentleman, you learned in the law, psychologists and pathologists, do me justice! Love led me to take the step I took; all my deeds were conditioned by it. God put it in my heart.' (von Krafft-Ebbing, 1892: 314). It is a chilling document to read and beside it the portrait of Stephen Gordon seems humane and generous. Interestingly, the role of the father is seen as highly significant in the development of the condition and there is much debate generally within the text about whether inversion is an acquired or congenital condition.

> The female urning, even when a little girl, presents the reverse. Her favourite place is the playground of boys. She seeks to rival them in their games.... Among many foolish things that her father encouraged in her was the fact that he brought her up as a boy, called her Sandor, allowed her to drive, ride and hunt.
> (von Krafft-Ebbing, 1892: 279–311)

There is a drive to fix all of this scientifically, a humiliating process that leads to the most ludicrous of claims:

> The upper jaw projects strikingly, its alveolar process projecting beyond the upper jaw about 0.5 centimetre. The position of the teeth is not fully normal. ... Genitals completely feminine ... labia minora have a cock's-comb-like form, and project under the labia majora. The clitoris is small and very sensitive ... vagina so narrow that the insertion of a membrum virile would be impossible ... there was a congenitally abnormal inversion of the sexual instinct, which, indeed, expressed itself, anthropologically, in anomolies of development of the body, depending upon great hereditary taint; further that the criminal acts of S. had their foundation in her abnormal and irresistable sexuality.
> (von Krafft-Ebbing, 1892: 316–17)

Who is Stephen Gordon, What is She?

Havelock Ellis, to whose views Radclyffe Hall was more sympathetic, is an improvement upon this but to a contemporary reader the difference is one of degree rather than kind. He is still, for example, capable of finding whistling useful in diagnosis:

> The frequent inability of male inverts to whistle was first pointed out by Ulrichs, and Hirschfield has found it in 23%. Many of my cases confess to this inability, while some of the women inverts can whistle admirably.
>
> (Ellis, 1924: 291)

Stephen Gordon, then, is clearly identified to the reader as a lesbian, although part of the interest in the novel is how long she remains in ignorance herself. The theme of naming is powerful in the novel, much of it concerned with the damage done to Stephen because of her inability to name herself or her condition. That loss of security and trust is compounded by the fear of naming demonstrated by others, notably her father and Puddle. As a heroine, however, there is a tension about where to place her: as a woman, as a lesbian, as a Gordon. Her greatest struggle is with being a woman, something that the novel sets in opposition to her lesbianism. The continuing tension in her character is that between the lesbian and the Gordon.

Stephen is a doomed and tragic figure from the outset and the tragedy of her lesbianism is that she loses Morton, the ancestral home. Morton is the touchstone against which all experiences are held. It is the thing she would give up for Angela; the source of deep hurt when she cannot take Mary there; the place she is banished from at the moment of truth between Lady Anna and herself.

Morton establishes Stephen in the social order, setting her at the heart of a moral world view that pervades, not just social life, but ways of writing about it. Whether it draws from the appeal of popular romance or the country-house novel, Stephen Gordon, through Morton, is at home in a conservative and idealized version of England. The opening of the novel ascribes virtues to the house that read as a gloss on Stephen's character: 'Dignity and pride without ostentation, self-

Who is Stephen Gordon, What is She?

assurance without arrogance, repose without inertia; and a gentle aloofness that, to those who know its spirit, but adds to its value.' (Hall, 1982: 7). Stephen does not simply live in Morton. What it represents has formed her: is a part of her. The social displacement and alienation that follow from her determination to be true to herself are registered through loss of place:

> The spirit of Morton would be part of her then, and would always remain somewhere deep down within her aloof and untouched by the years that must follow, by the stress and ugliness of life. In those after years certain scents would evoke it. Then that part of Stephen that she still shared with Morton would know what it was to feel terribly lonely, like a soul that wakes up to find itself wandering, unwanted, between the spheres.

(Hall, 1982: 32)

As a Gordon, Stephen is her father's daughter, claimed by what is male rather than what is female. Throughout the pregnancy, it is a son, rather than a child that is wanted. This desire is not uncommon, especially where there is land to inherit. Before she is born, then, Stephen has an allotted role within her family and society: one filled by sons, not daughters. The fact that Stephen is a girl does not deter Sir Philip. She is brought up as if she is the son he wants and will never have: 'You're all the son that I've got' (Hall, 82: 58).

Far from being a positive account of the ways in which gender identity is formed through culture rather than nature, his action finally becomes a source of guilt and doubt to him. He is saved from responsibility for his potentially irresponsible actions because the fiction makes clear that Stephen is receptive to a male bias in her upbringing and education. The unstated assumption being that a proper girl would have resisted by asserting her natural femininity.

The power of her father is extensive. He names her Stephen for the martyr whose truth was not believed, and witholds her name; as a lesbian. There is a certain irony in St Stephen also being the patron saint of headaches: Stephen Gordon has certainly caused lesbians a good few over the years! The

Who is Stephen Gordon, What is She?

problem she poses in sacrificing Mary at the end of the novel is an action that can be traced back to her conservatism, something her father inculcates.

Stephen venerates her parent's marriage. They create her image of a perfect union, sanctioned by God and society and rooted in love. Heterosexuality is at the root of Stephen Gordon's moral code; an:

> inherent respect of the normal . . . she must pay for the instinct which, in earliest childhood, had made her feel something akin to worship for the perfect thing which she had divined in the love that existed between her parents.
>
> (Hall,1982: 438)

It is this that underpins Stephen's manipulation of Mary, forcing her away, not on grounds of what is right or wrong, but of what is proper, what the world will sanction: 'children, a home that the world would respect, ties of affection that the world would hold sacred, the blessed security and the peace of being released from the world's persecution' (Hall, 1982: 438). Still with such a demonstration of the powers of patriarchy and the problematic nature of Stephen Gordon's action and motives, she endures as a heroine for lesbians. A positive example as well as a warning. How does she achieve this?

Appalling as the ending of the novel is, there is scope within it, and within the highly determined character of Stephen Gordon, for contradiction and complexity. Stephen Gordon exhibits a passion and defiance that lesbians need. She presents us with one of the few opportunities to participate in public discourse. Reading is an important source of knowledge and inspiration to lesbians, being one of the few cultural media to which there is access. Stephen's assertion that her love for Angela is on a par with that of her parents is shocking; the confidence with which she asserts initially what she can give Mary over what any man could, are all acts of enormous courage. But perhaps more important than balancing empowering acts and statements against disempowering ones, is to recognize that Stephen Gordon's greatest virtue is that she grows into, not out of, her sexual identity.

Who is Stephen Gordon, What is She?

Her maturity as a person: the extent to which she defines and begins to execute a life work for herself; the degree to which she establishes a social equilibrium; are linked to her awareness about her sexuality. She is shown as capable of change, able to adapt and develop. By the end of the novel the morality she embodies, which dictates the tragic outcome of the novel, is described as: 'An added burden it was, handed down by the silent but watchful founders of Morton. She must pay for the instinct' (Hall, 1982: 438).

The virtue has become ambiguous, the price extremely high. It is not just Stephen Gordon who pays it either. Generations of readers, both heterosexual and lesbian, have had to contend with Stephen Gordon, a character who has sometimes exerted too strong and singular an influence over what it means to be a lesbian.

Chapter Two

STEPHEN GORDON AND OTHER PEOPLE IN HER LIFE

THE SINGLE most important person in Stephen Gordon's life is her author, Radclyffe Hall. Stephen rarely slips that leash – her every move and feeling pre-planned and charted, leading inexorably towards martyrdom. 'You were made for a martyr!' says Valerie Seymour, in exasperation as Stephen wilfully sets in train the series of events that will drive Mary into the arms of Martin Hallam. And so she is, a making grounded in the measure of her difference from other people.

Stephen Gordon's life, from before conception through to maturity, stresses interdependance. The very isolation she is forced into underlines the necessity and value of those connections. Over and over, it is the denial of society that measures the individual suffering experienced by Stephen 'and all her kind'.

The language used to describe Stephen is from the outset, that of alienation and difference. She is 'Queer', 'Awkward', 'Strange', 'Not as other children', described in relation to loneliness and aloneness. The text requires such singularity from Stephen Gordon. She exemplifies the damaging isolation against which, finally, the text pits itself. She is, however, never as alone as she seems, although often her spiritual loneliness is emphasized precisely through her social connections, duties, and obligations. All the same, there are points in the text where a certain wilfulness seems to be at work, obscuring real and vital connections between Stephen and other women.

The isolation she experiences does not have a fixed quality.

Stephen Gordon and Other People

The text argues that at times it can be unhealthy, at other times, vital. By the end of the novel, the ascetic isolation implied in renouncing Mary, seems entirely appropriate to Stephen Gordon's near-visionary state. Only when free of any personal, everyday claims upon her is she able to receive 'those countless others ... the fierce yet helpless children who would clamour in vain for their right to salvation' (Hall, 82: 446). Isolation here has become that of the mystic or saint, whose withdrawal from the world is the often painful means to express greater love and faith in it. Stephen, in taking up the cause of her kind, becomes not just a supplicant to God, but as one with God herself. 'They would turn first to God, and then to the world, and then to her. They would cry out accusing: "We have asked for bread; will you give us a stone?"' (Hall, 82: 446).

Before she reaches this state of grace, however, Stephen's experience of isolation undergoes many transformations. This emphasizes the importance of change within the novel.

Early childhood is in many ways idyllic. Stephen is her father's favoured child, petted and indulged. She has freedom and privileges. Yet for all that, she is a lonely child, and a lonelier adolescent, with the precocity of having always had adult companions.

The isolation she embraces with such zeal after the departure from her life of Martin Hallam and Angela Crossby, who each in their own way appeared to promise the possibility of connection and partnership, is clearly disapproved of. It diminishes Stephen, physically and mentally, and is only redeemed by her writing. It is only when the writing falters that action is taken. From here on, there is a constant struggle between the need for isolation as the precondition for writing and the tendency for that to become obsessional, overriding all other necessities and preoccupations.

The conflict between her work and personal life reflects the influences that stressed purposeful work as her salvation. First her father, then Puddle, encouraged this until, fully internalized, it is Stephen's own sense of destiny. There is no obligation or precedent for Stephen to work; the writing she dedicated herself to is both a gift and a solution to her problem

Stephen Gordon and Other People

of identity. 'Writing ... it was like the lifting of a load from the spirit, it brought with it a sense of relief, of assuagement. One could say things in writing without feeling self-conscious, without feeling shy and ashamed and foolish' (Hall, 82: 68).

Lesbianism is at the root of Stephen's isolation. It distances her from social life and ease and she comes to believe herself the only one ever to have felt that dislocation. In some respects the text demands that Stephen experiences herself like this in order to fully meditate upon the nature of lesbianism. It is also, as far as readers are concerned, in Radclyffe Hall's interests to focus attention upon one impressive figure. However, there runs through the entire novel a kind of counter-commentary that emphasizes the history and multiplicity of lesbian existence at precisely those moments when Stephen's isolation is being wrung for all the pity and sympathy it can muster. This discourse is almost more important than the main text's preoccupation with Stephen's isolation, precisely because it insists upon a variety of lesbian experience.

Significant in this respect are the periods during childhood when vague hints and presentiments are scattered between passages describing Stephen's unwillingness to wear frocks and to prefer feminine games or behaviour. Her mother is shown to be perplexed, aware only that her child is not like others, presumably also not as Anna remembers her own girlhood. Sir Philip, in contrast, is not only aware of her difference from other children, he also has access to knowledge, symbolized by his study and the books in it, that explain and confirm his suspicions. His actions isolate Stephen within the family and profoundly disturbs her sense of self-identity but they hint, too, at others. If there are books written before Stephen is born, before she has grown up, then she is born into history, one of others, one of many.

It seems incredible, at times, that Stephen should remain so naïve about herself for so long. Presumably, this insistence upon her innocence helps diminish any hint of viciousness or depravity. Its price is paranoia, which forms the context for all her relationships and provides one of the novel's major themes: that of persecution. Early on in the novel, Stephen refers to:

Stephen Gordon and Other People

'Her old suspicion, the suspicion that had haunted her ever since childhood – she would fancy that people were laughing at her. So sensitive was she, that a half-heard sentence, a word, a glance, made her inwardly crumble' (Hall, 82: 73). This acute sensitivity is both a rational and irrational response for Stephen. Her striking appearance certainly causes public comment, often unflattering. Out shopping in London, 'a man, laughed and nudged his companion. "Look at that! What is it?"' (Hall, 82: 164). Much later in the novel, when Martin Hallam, accompanying Mary and Stephen around Paris, leaves Stephen alone to dance with Mary she is 'Uncomfortably conscious of the interest she aroused by reason of her clothes and her isolation' (Hall 82: 425).

Her acute sensitivity to real looks and comments is only part of the picture. Stephen also imagines them. This reflects the insecurity experienced by those who know themselves to be different, and know to fear the reactions the discovery of that difference can provoke. The unrelenting persecution Stephen Gordon either observes, imagines, or experiences, takes to the extreme something known personally to lesbians. The exaggeration is a means of exorcism and vindication, a reminder that the present is not so bad, but also making that link to the past. It also makes the point that lesbian lives are fundamentally insecure and vulnerable, not because of anything in the nature of lesbians, but rather because of the pressures and scrutiny under which they are put.

Stephen Gordon's isolation is contradictory in other respects too. She relies entirely on servants; not just for the practical, menial tasks in life but also for her moral, spiritual, and companionate needs.

Stephen's sense of family is in her relations with Puddle, Mlle Duphot and Pierre, Pauline, and Adele. The relationship is unequal, but reciprocal. They nurture her, Stephen is allowed largesse: cars are made available, weddings paid for, and favours bestowed. This is in marked contrast to Stephen's own blood relations, where the story is one of estrangement. She is the last of the Gordons, and this position both sustains and undermines her.

Stephen Gordon and Other People

Much of Stephen's strength is drawn from Morton; it roots her in time and history; her banishment is the highest index of her suffering. And Morton, the house, is represented by:

> The funny old portraits of Gordons – men long dead and gone but still wonderfully living, since their thoughts had fashioned the comeliness of Morton; since their loves had made children from father to son – from father to son until the advent of Stephen.
>
> (Hall, 82: 103)

It is Stephen who spoils the line, brings it to an end, under the unsmiling gaze of these forbears, whose lack of mirth is attributed thus: 'as though they were thinking of Stephen' (Hall, 82: 86).

Beyond this familial network, however, the world in general is perceived as being and often is, hostile. On various occasions it is precisely the family connection that softens and makes possible otherwise difficult situations. So, for example, when Stephen endures the embarrassment of trying to purchase Angela a pearl ring, her redemption lies in lighting, by chance, upon her father's jeweller.

He recognizes her and tells the story of her father buying her mother's engagement ring. The sense of respect, for the past and for her father's role, overrides the social awkwardness of one woman buying an expensive ring for another, upon which Stephen floundered in the other jewellers. Stephen's identification as lover, with her father, strengthens her and helps her to ignore the social disapproval she had formerly been so conscious of:

> As she walked down the street she was lost in thought, so that if people stared she no longer noticed. In her ears kept sounding those words from the past, those words of her father's when long, long ago he too had been a young lover: 'She's so pure that only the purest stones are fit to touch her fingers.'
>
> (Hall, 82: 167)

Stephen's ability to fend off such social hostility comes slowly and painfully.

Stephen Gordon and Other People

One of the most enduring relationships in *The Well of Loneliness* is the one that Stephen Gordon has with God. It is not an easy relationship, but it is never dispensable. Even when Stephen, as a character, is experiencing a crisis of faith that distances her from God, the text never lets go of the broadly religious organizing structure. Addressing God, as Stephen does loudly and relentlessly throughout the novel, she is also addressing herself, the God within her.

The Well of Loneliness is a profoundly moral book and that morality is carried by the character of Stephen Gordon. It operates in relation to her: how she is treated, how she behaves. There is never any chance of forgetting that behind Stephen Gordon's moral code stands God. That the novel dares to speak in the name of God for and about homosexuality was later to constitute its immorality.

It is surely no accident that Stephen is born at Christmas: there is a high degree of identification with the figure of Christ, which reaches its climax in the final pages of the novel. There, the visionary hallucinations Stephen undergoes are presented as a form of crucifixion. The pain she experiences, her own pain, is the accumulated misery and suffering of the world's homosexuals: 'all the misery at Alec's. And the press and clamour of those countless others. She raised her arms, trying to ward them off, but they closed in and in: 'You dare not dismiss us!' (Hall, 82: 446).

It is through taking their suffering as her own that Stephen is able, finally, to articulate the message that the whole book has, in one form or another, been moving towards to: 'Acknowledge us, oh God, before the whole world. Give us also the right to our existence!' (Hall, 82: 447).

In addition to borrowing from the life of Christ to structure the progress of the book, the language borrows heavily from biblical constructions and inflections. These borrowings are awkward, adding a sententiousness to the work.

So why is the novel so closely tied to religious themes? The explanation is partly autobiographical. Radclyffe Hall was a convert to Catholicism, a conversion that was part of her commitment to Ladye (Mabel Batten), one of the more

13

Stephen Gordon and Other People

significant lesbian relationships of her life. It is not stretching the imagination too far to suppose that for Radclyffe Hall, Catholicism was intimately bound up with living as a lesbian. Her sincerity in believing lesbianism to be part of God's plan never wavered, although this belief would have been severely tested by the Catholic Church's illiberal teaching on homosexuality. *The Well of Loneliness* involves a very protracted debate about what sort of lesbian to be: it never admits the argument about whether or not to be one.

In refusing to acknowledge the argument that lesbianism is aberrant, the devil's work, Radclyffe Hall makes an absolute argument for the godliness of her condition. This constitutes the soundest base from which to plead the case for social tolerance. The case for tolerance is pitted against decadence, a charge against lesbianism that Radclyffe Hall is at great pains to refute. She is fully, judgementally aware of the decadence that flourishes alongside lesbian culture. She asks us to condemn it, and in doing so to recognize how social exclusion and disapproval creates the very immorality it condemns. Against decadence, Hall asserts the entire weight of the conservative Christianity that floods the book. Her sense of the sacred extends beyond things of the spirit to the land and social relations embodied in Morton. This is partly the product of a deeply traditionalist social conservatism and partly a means to express the profound difference between that world, and the men and women who are of it, and the decadent, immoral lives they will be forced into if denied the opportunity to carry out their social destiny. By setting lesbianism within nature as part of God's plan, to deny its right to exist is to go against God.

God performs two functions in the development of Stephen Gordon's character, both of which operate in relation to solitude and isolation. Initially, when Stephen is socially isolated, her dialogues with God are a means of identifying and exploring the conflicting pressures upon her. The discussion, for the reader as much as for Stephen, becomes something other than introspective. This gives the issue power and permanence. God is a sounding board, both standing in for other people, mediating her aloneness, and something to rail at: for being

Stephen Gordon and Other People

born a girl, not a boy; for the difficulties with Martin Hallam, with Angela Crossby.

God, then, becomes both a relationship in its own right and a context for all her other relationships. It is interesting to track the different forms that takes and also to see how God comes in and out of focus, depending on the degree of contentment Stephen has with the rest of her life.

Stephen is not born into a particularly devout household. Out of pleasure at his wife's pregnancy, 'Sir Philip went to church, which was seldom his custom' (Hall, 82: 9). Lady Anna comes to hear Stephen's bedtime prayers 'As custom demanded' (Hall, 82: 18).

Later, as Stephen's character develops, and her difference becomes an issue for her parents, they each in quite different ways invoke the morality of Christianity and the authority of God. Her father does so with some measure of compassion for Stephen, albeit misplaced. When Stephen finally gains the courage to ask: 'Is there anything strange about me, Father?' (Hall, 82: 104), he lies, fudging her question; moving it away from her initial focus on her feelings about men to the more general statement that marriage isn't the only career for a woman, announcing that he plans to send her to Oxford. This exchange is presented in a complicated way. That her father acts out of love, out of his pity for Stephen is emphasized and acknowledged with authorial generosity: 'the lie was still bitter to his spirit as he sat there, and he covered his face for the shame that was in him – but because of the love that was in him he wept' (Hall, 82: 105). At the same time, he is not spared any contempt, being described as: 'frightened, a coward ... inwardly grovelling ... smiling right into her eyes he lied glibly' (Hall, 82: 104–5), descriptions that sit uneasily with the motif of honour running through Stephen's relationship with her father.

God stands in the midst of his behaviour. He is angry, puzzled as to which sins of the fathers are now being visited upon Stephen: 'He wanted to cry out against God for this thing; he wanted to cry out: "You have maimed my Stephen! What had I done or my father before me" ' (Hall, 82: 104).

Stephen Gordon and Other People

His overt sense of Stephen as a maimed, imperfect being, albeit made by God, is somehow more shocking than her mother's unambiguous revulsion. Partly, of course, this stems from a fury that he arrogates to himself the power to tell Stephen what he suspects about her and decides not to. He acts selfishly, weakly turning back to God: 'I will not tell her. You cannot ask it – there are some things that even God should not ask' (Hall, 82: 105).

The weakness of Sir Philip's recourse to God in justifying a moral cowardice is underlined, not just by the presentation of this episode, but also with reference to his more general Christianity. It is, for him, less a code of moral and spiritual values than a spectacle and show: he attends church during his wife's pregnancy, he makes a ritual of Christmas: 'loved the old German custom which would seem to insist that even the aged be as children and play with God on His birthday' (Hall, 82: 86).

This particular Christmas, of Stephen's eighteenth birthday, is intended both to endear and underline the interconnectedness of the Gordons with the fabric of social life, tradition, and rank: obligation, duty, and service. All the same, in a book that strives after large, moral themes, it is damning.

Anna's sense of God is somehow more palatable, despite the hostility towards Stephen that she justifies on the grounds of religion. She is, in her own terms, honest. Anna prays and, when her relationship with Stephen first starts to break down, her prayers are for help in resolving that. Chilling as the sentiment is, her sincerity in facing and seeking to overcome it are, at this stage, unarguable: ' "Give me peace," she would entreat, "and enlighten my spirit, so that I may learn how to love my own child" ' (Hall, 82: 80).

Her struggle is unsuccessful. She never can resolve her feelings towards Stephen. Much later, when the affair with Angela Crossby is brought to her attention, the full fury of that struggle descends upon Stephen. Anna is vindicated; the fault is Stephen's, not hers. And Lady Anna has God on her side:

It is you who are unnatural, not I. And this thing that you are is

> a sin against creation ... this unspeakable outrage that you call
> love ... coming from you they are vile and filthy words of
> corruption – against nature, against God who created nature.
>
> (Hall, 82: 203)

It is Anna who, at this pivotal point where Stephen is forced to leave the familiar and protected environment of Morton, sets out the terms of engagement for the rest of the novel. Is Stephen to be counted as one with, or apart from, the natural, God-given order?

What characterizes both her parent's relationship to God, in terms of Stephen, is that they never entreat God on her behalf. They rail at God, they get angry because of Stephen; they condemn Stephen in God's name. Never do they ask for God's intercession: for mercy. In this way, her parents stand outside the morality that the book strives towards. Significantly, her alternative family, that of the paid governesses who become her companions, do not fail Stephen in this respect.

When Mlle Duphot leaves and Stephen is tidying the schoolroom preparatory to the arrival of Puddle, which signals the end of 'irresponsible childhood' (Hall, 82: 68), Stephen finds a little piety card, inscribed with the words 'Priez pour ma Stevenne'. The strangeness of her charge has not escaped Mlle Duphot, but in her response, Stephen's interests are uppermost. Interestingly, the French language allows for the feminization of her name, hinting at the changes France will bring. Later, living in Paris, Stephen encounters Mlle Duphot again. To begin with, all goes well, but the repercussions of the incident with Lady Massey lead Stephen to reduce the frequency of their visits on the grounds that: 'We're here under false pretences. If she knew what we were, she'd have none of us either' (Hall, 82: 385).

The vignette that follows illustrates both how Stephen and Mary are set firmly towards their fate and indicates how Stephen's failure to trust contributes to that disaster. Mlle Duphot puts their withdrawal down to Stephen's fame. Her blind sister divines another reason: 'I can feel great desolation in Stevenne – and some of the youngness has gone from Mary. What can it be? My fingers grow blind when I ask them the

Stephen Gordon and Other People

cause of that desolation' (Hall 82: 386). Mlle Duphot will pray for them both, 'to the Sacred Heart which comprehends all things' (Hall 82: 386), and the author reminds us here that Mlle Duphot's own heart would also have made that effort to understand. Instead of the earlier gap between God and the world, we have at this stage of the novel, hints at bridges between the two.

Puddle, the companion of her late teens and twenties, is not above arguing with God from her sense of Stephen as a 'sorely afflicted creature' (Hall, 82: 217), yet she too, like Mlle Duphot, prays for Stephen, each of them quite confident that she has a claim upon God.

Stephen's engagement with God, in relation to other people, is not consistent throughout the novel. It is at its fiercest during her childish infatuation with Collins; with Martin Hallam there is still passion, but it is intellectually based: with Angela Crossby a period of bleak estrangement takes over, which is only displaced when Mary Llewellyn enters Stephen's life. It is significant that during the relationship with Mary, the only references to God are those that speak of pleasure and glory. Finally, as the pressures upon them mount, God comes sharply back into focus for Stephen.

Stephen's precocious attachment to Collins lays very early the foundations of the adult Stephen's sense of what it is to love. Love is bound up with pain. However ridiculous Stephen's desire to bear the pain of Collins' housemaid's knee may seem, the seriousness with which she accepts and understands why 'Jesus had chosen to bear pain for sinners, when he might have called up all those angels! (Hall, 82: 18) is a characteristic that will come into its own as Stephen matures. The earnest desire 'to wash Collins in my blood, Lord Jesus – I would like very much to be a saviour to Collins' (Hall, 82: 18), will, likewise, return in the novel's closing pages. There is a sincerity about Stephen Gordon's commitment to the expression of love as suffering, despite the appalling class prejudice that sanctions such an orgy of self-sacrifice for a woman whose first name the young Stephen apparently does not know.

These intense exchanges with the Lord are conducted in

18

Stephen Gordon and Other People

private and distance Stephen from her mother. While her mother is listening to her prayers, she conducts herself meekly. After she departs, Stephen prays: 'in good earnest – with such fervour, indeed, that she dripped perspiration in a veritable orgy of prayer' (Hall, 82: 18).

Later, she will be admonished by her nurse, not her mother: 'Not so loud, Miss Stephen! Pray slower, and don't shout at the Lord, He won't like it! (Hall, 82: 34).

Some ten years later, Stephen no longer reproaches the Lord Jesus because: 'He wants all the pain for Himself; He won't share it! (Hall, 82: 27), instead she doubts His existence. Her conversations with Martin Hallam revolve around the spirituality of nature and its transcendant qualities. Martin's ideas about trees are identical to the view of homosexual existence portrayed by the book. It is because of these trees that he believes in God:

> They're all twisted and crippled; it hurts me to see them, yet they go on patiently doing their bit – have you ever thought about the enormous courage of trees? I have, and it seems to be amazing. The Lord dumps them down and they've just got to stick it, no matter what happens – that must need some courage!
>
> (Hall, 82: 93)

The crisis that attends Martin's declaration of love is less about God, than about Stephen's sense of being outside nature. Events overtake her, the death of her father plunges her into a deeper crisis. Out hunting, in an epiphany of identification with the fox, she rediscovers God by recognizing that in its extremity, this creature seeks for its Maker. This sanctions Stephen, in her own extremity, to acknowledge: 'her mighty need to believe, a need that was stronger than physical pain, being born of the pain of the spirit' (Hall, 82: 124).

A year later, Angela Crossby enters Stephen's life and events occur that reduce Stephen to the nadir of her affinity with God. The crisis Stephen experiences, coming to understand her feelings for Angela in the context of rivalry with Roger Antrim, is counterpointed to Violet Antrim's engagement:

Stephen Gordon and Other People

There they would kneel, the young newly wed, ardent yet
sanctified by a blessing, so that all, or at least nearly all, they
would do, must be considered both natural and pleasing to a
God in the image of man created. And the fact that this God, in a
thoughtless moment, had created in His turn those pitiful
thousands who must stand forever outside His blessing, would
in no way disturb the large congregation or their white surpliced
pastor.'

(Hall, 82: 189–90)

There is a tension here, the criticism not just of people who do
not acknowledge God's work in the creation of homosexuals,
but also of God, for whom they exist as an act of
'thoughtlessness'. Much later in the novel, when Jean and
Adèle are married from Stephen's house in Paris, there is less
railing against the unfairness of God and hypocrisy of society.
Instead, the marriage ceremony invokes a sadness that actually
draws Stephen and Mary closer. 'As the twilight gradually
merged into dusk, these three must huddle ever closer together –
David with his head upon Mary's lap, Mary with her head
against Stephen's shoulder' (Hall, 82: 400).

Stephen does not debate with God during her relationship
with Angela. She deals directly with people: Angela, Ralph, her
mother. God returns when Stephen confronts the loss both of
Angela and of Morton. In her father's study she reads the books
he had read; learns the truth about herself he has denied her.
Her response is one of distress: but she addresses her father not
God: 'God's cruel; He let us get flawed in the making' (Hall, 82:
207).

That sense of flaw, of being less than perfect, is constant
throughout the novel and represents one of its most difficult
aspects. The scene is one of high suspense and melodrama; she
turns to the Bible, 'demanding a sign from heaven – nothing
less' (Hall, 82: 238). The Bible falls open at the story of Cain
and Stephen becomes hysterical, taking this as her sign:
'Completely hopeless and beaten, rocking her body backwards
and forwards with a kind of abrupt yet methodical rhythm:
"And the Lord set a mark upon Cain, upon Cain"' (Hall, 82:
207).

Stephen Gordon and Other People

For the rest of the novel, Stephen carries that mark of Cain. It defines her sense of what lesbian existence is, and as such, is extremely negative. What Stephen is unable to grasp, although the reader may make the distinction, is that Cain was culpable, Cain killed Abel. Stephen's only culpable act is to love: something that both she and the narrator keep firmly out of the realm of sin.

From this point on, it is the world rather than God that occupies Stephen, so that when the sense of engagement with God re-emerges towards the end of the novel, it holds all the power of suffering, tribulation, and pleasure of that world. Stephen's third book, written during her relationship with Mary, is a great success, harking back to and fulfilling the promise of her first. Puddle's assertion that: 'Work's your only weapon. Make the world respect you as you can do through your work; it's the surest harbour of refuge for your friend, the only harbour' (Hall, 82: 343) appears to hold true. Stephen's success draws respect from family, friends, and strangers alike. Violet wishes to cultivate her now, her mother writes to her at length. She feels confident, of herself and her relationship with Mary: 'Gazing at Mary, with very bright eyes. . . . "Nothing shall ever hurt you" she would promise, feeling wonderfully self-sufficient and strong, wonderfully capable of protecting' (Hall, 82: 371).

The height of this good fortune comes when, on holiday in Italy, Stephen and Mary are befriended by Lady Massey and her daughter, Agnes. Lady Massey:

> petted Mary, and mothered her as though she were a child, and soon she was mothering Stephen also. She would say: 'I seem to have found two new children', and Stephen, who was in the mood to feel touched, grew quite attached to this ageing woman.
> (Hall, 82: 372)

The holiday ends, the friendship continues. Stephen entertains them while in Paris, and there are frequent letters once Lady Massey returns to England. They are invited to spend Christmas with her. The pleasures of this friendship opens old wounds and losses: Stephen is envious of the social

Stephen Gordon and Other People

respectability of land and family; Mary of the ease and security of living a normal life. Stephen:

> must envy these commonplace men and women with their ridiculous shooting stocks, their smiling fiances; their husbands; their wives; their estates, and their well-cared for, placid children. Mary would sometimes look over her shoulder with a new and perhaps rather wistful interest.
>
> (Hall, 82: 373)

At these moments of distress, the invitation, to spend Christmas at Branscombe Court is like a talisman. It makes them both feel better, despite the reminder of exile from Morton it brings: The visit: 'Appeared like the first fruits of toil; to Mary like the gateway into an existence that must be very safe and reassuring' (Hall, 82: 374).

It is almost inevitable that it doesn't take place. A letter arrives just as they are about to leave speaking of: 'Rumours that have reached me about you and Mary – certain things that I don't want to enter into' (Hall, 82: 374). The shock of this rejection does not bring them closer together. They each find quite different ways of coping. Mary throws herself wholeheartedly into the lesbian nightlife; Stephen becomes preoccupied with Catholicism. By the end of the novel, Stephen has completely taken into herself a sense of mission.

The preoccupation builds slowly. It is first intimated during a recital of negro spirituals given by two of Jamie's fellow students. Riven as the scene is by gross assertions such as: 'His eyes had the patient, questioning expression common to the eyes of most animals and to those of all slowly evolving races' (Hall, 82: 366), it nevertheless speaks of spiritual enlightenment and makes a claim for the communality of their interests, an idea as progressive for its time as her views on race were commonplace.

> all the terrible, aching, homesick hope that is born of the infinite pain of the spirit, seemed to break from this man and shake those who listened, so that they sat with bent heads and clasped hands – they who were also among the hopeless sat with bent heads and

Stephen Gordon and Other People

> clasped hands as they listened. . . . Even Valérie Seymour forgot
> to be pagan.
>
> (Hall, 82: 366)

The recital ends with a song, the refrain of which is: 'Didn't my
Lord deliver Daniel, Then why not every man?' (Hall, 82: 367).
This carries over from the context of American slavery and
becomes a challenge and a rallying call in the book for all the
oppressed. 'Yes, but how long, O Lord, how long?' floats into
the text, spoken by neither Stephen nor the singers. It brings
that waiting into the novel itself, marking the first stage of
Stephen's journey to conversion.

Stephen's progress towards faith is next carried forward by
Wanda, another of the Parisian lesbians. Wanda has a
passionate temperament, is an artist, and is prone to excessive
drinking. Her Polish Catholic background is exemplary: she is
the sister to three brothers, all of them priests. In a penitent
mood, she renounces drink and her faith helps to sustain her in
doing that. She introduces Stephen to Sacre Coeur and provides
a focus for her new interest in religion. This is shown to be
quite out of keeping with the preoccupations of the rest of their
circle. Mary interrupts Wanda's attempts to explain her reasons
for having to leave Poland by starting up the gramophone and
encouraging everyone to dance.

Wanda talks to Stephen, unable to communicate Catholicism's real spirituality, and takes her with her to visit Sacré
Coeur. It is these visits, the meditation upon Christ's suffering
that clarifies Stephen's sense of destiny.

Early on, love was identified with suffering for Stephen.
Here, in the vision of the sacred heart, she finds relief for her
own suffering and hope for others. Stephen has always been
fearless; courage is her most stalwart virtue. In the face of God,
her fearlessness takes two forms. Firstly, she likens the
procession of the priest with the monstrance to the procession
of lepers. It's a daring image, condensing the history of Christ,
outcast and shunned, with that of another outcast group whom
he had the power to heal. Because it is Stephen, standing
thinking these thoughts, the image has also to include both her

Stephen Gordon and Other People

and Wanda, supplicants for compassion: 'We are two yet we stand for many. Our name is legion.... Thus the Prisoner of love Who could never break free while one spiritual leper remained to be healed, passed by on His patient way, heavy-laden' (Hall, 82: 382–3).

Her second act of fearlessness is that, unlike Wanda who falls to her knees and 'cowered at the sight of her own salvation' (Hall, 82: 438); Stephen remains standing, respectful, but facing her Lord, claiming an equality. It is, so to speak, on her feet rather than on her knees, that Stephen embraces God and her duty towards him. Stephen, in exploring her response to God, is at pains to distance herself from what she sees as a kind of self-indulgence. God is not so much sanctuary for Stephen as the impetus to action: 'Unless there's a God, where do some of us find even the little courage we possess?' (Hall, 82: 428).

When she does seek sanctuary, stumbling into Sacre Coeur just after she has reached her decision that Mary must go to Martin, it is a moment of anticlimax. She stands in front of the statue that had been the focus of the trips with Wanda, the little silver Christ with the: 'patient gesture of supplication ... without finding anything to say, embarrassed as one so frequently is in the presence of somebody else's sorrow. For herself she felt nothing, neither pity nor regret' (Hall, 82: 441–2).

God will not deliver Stephen from her individual pain, only urge her to make connections on the largest scale between herself, the oppressed, and God: a retreat that must, finally, send her back.

In her childhood and teenage years, Stephen is socially alienated. She cannot form attachments with or enjoy the pastimes of her contemporaries. This awkwardness begins early on: 'Her relations with other children were peculiar, she thought so herself and so did the children ... a high-spirited child she should have been popular, and yet she was not' (Hall, 82: 43). She is forced by her parents and against her will to visit and play with the Antrim children, Violet and Roger. Stephen lacks social grace. She is clumsy and tongue-tied, aware of her feet being too large, possessing an appetite to match Roger's

Stephen Gordon and Other People

rather than Violet's. She is the source of some amusement to Mrs Antrim, as well as a reinforcement of her pride in Violet. Colonel Antrim, who has a soft spot for Stephen, is excluded from these domestic scenes that so undermine Stephen.

Violet and Roger are presented as a typical girl and boy, which further enhances Stephen's uneasy position somewhere in between. In fact they are both extremes, possessing almost caricatured qualities of femininity and masculinity. It is hard for a modern reader not to see Stephen's reaction to Violet as quite healthy. The narrative tone adopted towards Violet is merciless. She is shown as being silly and affected, boasting of female accomplishments she wants to be thought of as possessing: 'People said: "Look at Violet, she's like a little mother; its so touching to see that instinct in a child!" Then Violet would become still more touching' (Hall, 82: 44). Violet is exposed, in her false seeking after adult approval, and the maternal instinct is revealed as a conditioned reflex rather than as an innate drive.

Stephen's relationship with Violet is characterized by frustration at being left to play with her, rather than the sort of games she really likes, which only Roger plays. It indicates Stephen's estrangement from femininity, the message that a woman is not a positive thing to be and confirms, at this very early age, a motif running through the whole novel, namely, Stephen's struggles to be a man. Roger Antrim is just as, if not more unpleasant than his sister. He is a bully, not very accomplished at games and rather slow off the mark. Although Stephen hates him, 'Her loathing was increased by a most humiliating consciousness of envy' (Hall, 82: 44).

The conflict here is much sharper than that between Violet and Stephen, another instance of Stephen Gordon's orientation towards men. It is men she looks to, measures herself against, and aspires towards. It is in their freedom that she finds an image of the naturalness denied her: She:

> Envied his right to climb trees and play cricket and football – his right to be perfectly natural; above all she envied his splendid conviction that being a boy constitued a privilege in life; she

Stephen Gordon and Other People

could well understand that conviction, but this only increased her envy.

(Hall, 82: 44)

So, Roger and Stephen fight with each other, physically and verbally, with Roger seeing in her, 'a kind of rival, a kind of intruder into his especial province (Hall, 82: 44), and yet retaining here, as he will later in far more serious circumstances, the advantage of his sex over her. He goads her about the hunt and realizing that, unusually, she has risen to his bait, presses on. It is the insult to her mother, rather than those to herself that provokes:

> 'And my mother said,' he continued more loudly, 'that your mother must be funny to allow you to do it; she said it was horrid to let girls ride that way ... she said that she'd have thought that your mother had more sense; she said that it wasn't modest.'

(Hall, 82:49)

To defend her mother's honour, she challenges Roger to a fight. 'I don't fight with girls!' remarks Roger, sauntering off.

Stephen's actions are justifiable, heroic even, yet the language used to describe her entirely undercuts this. 'Large splendour ... like some primitive thing conceived in a turbulent age of transition' (Hall, 82: 49). This incident leads to an argument between Stephen's parents about her upbringing, an argument her mother loses. Stephen is not shown in company again until she is a teenager, her life stays rooted in the world that is Morton; of family, servants, and animals.

All teenagers experience anxiety during the difficult transition from child to adult, and the heightening of sexual difference and attraction it usually entails. This period of Stephen's life is told from the inside; whereas at earlier and later points in the novel, things will be revealed to us dramatically, through interactions between people, much of this crisis is communicated through Stephen's soliloquies and the reported comments of other people. This heightens the effect of isolation, which is how Stephen experiences this phase of her life.

Stephen Gordon and Other People

As Stephen develops, her physique is one that men do not find attractive. She is tall, slim, and has the facial characteristics of her father. It is: 'A fine face, very pleasing, yet with something about it that went ill with the hats on which Anna insisted' (Hall, 82: 70). There are constant battles between Anna and Stephen about what she should wear and a sense of despair, from both of them, that nothing ever looks quite as it should. Stephen returns the problem to herself: 'Am I queer looking or not? She would wonder' (Hall, 82: 70), staring into her mirror.

Stephen out in company is a source of anxiety to her mother. Her alienation takes different forms with women as opposed to men, but applies equally to both.

Stephen is not 'one of the girls'. She lacks the ease with them, and with femininity, to gossip and enjoy intimacy with the other young women of her set. They have nothing in common with each other and do not really interest her. But she is also excluded by them. They recognize her difference and close ranks against it, finding Stephen's primness:

> queer and absurd – after all, between girls – surely everyone knew that at times one ought not to get one's feet wet.... To see Stephen Gordon's expression of horror if one so much as threw out a hint on the subject was to feel that the thing must be in some way shameful, a kind of disgrace, a humiliation.
>
> (Hall, 82: 73–4)

Again, there is the devaluing, the denial of the female body. There is a very fine line between Stephen's inability to come to terms with femininity, which is critiqued throughout the novel and shown as having been acquired rather than as natural, and her femaleness, which is often, through references to the 'No-man's-land of sex', implied to be inappropriate to describe her.

For all that the girls bore Stephen, she envies them. She wants the security that being part of their circle would bring: 'While despising these girls, yet she longed to be like them.... It would suddenly strike her that they seemed very happy, very sure of themselves...so secure in their feminine conclaves' (Hall, 82: 74).

Stephen's actual interests are much more akin to the men's but her problems in becoming 'one of the girls', are as nothing

Stephen Gordon and Other People

beside those of being 'one of the lads'. She cannot meet men on equal terms and it is they who determine the inequality. She prefers their company, having more in common with them and finding their blunt, open outlook more congenial. But she antagonizes men. It is important that there is this antagonism. It is not just that she isn't liked or found attractive by them: 'Men found her too clever if she ventured to expound, and too dull if she suddenly subsided into shyness.... Shy though she might be, they sensed this presumption; it annoyed them, it made them feel defensive' (Hall, 82: 74–5).

The antagonism has two sources. It is partly that Stephen does not behave as women, to their mind, should: she is too independent and eschews the games and artifice of femininity. But there is also, as there was with Roger Antrim, the sense that Stephen is a rival, intruding on their territory. An image from the natural world, of oaks and ivy, is used to symbolize the relations between the sexes and Stephen is suspected of having: 'Something of the acorn about her' (Hall, 82: 75).

Despite femininity being shown as artificial, acquired behaviour, at the same time it provides the inflexible rules of social conduct. Stephen's discomfort is heightened in these situations because they are inescapable. To participate in social life, Stephen must be partnered. She thinks of those men as 'victims', as bound to her as she is to them. They focus very sharply for Stephen the issue of freedom, much as her envy of Roger Antrim did: 'If I were he I wouldn't be a bore, I could just be myself. I'd feel perfectly natural' (Hall, 82: 76). There is again the ambiguity as to whether being a man would constitute the natural self, i.e., whether Stephen's natural self is male; or whether the power that men have would enable her natural self, whatever it is, to be expressed. Seen against other people of her age and class, we have an acute sense of Stephen's distance from them. She clearly does not belong, but where she might belong is harder to establish at this point. The narrative does not pin her down. Instead, we are made to consider how far the social and the natural combine to form her personality; how much of what Stephen is, is owed to each.

Stephen's contemporaries do not form relationships with her;

Stephen Gordon and Other People

she does not learn with and from them how to conduct herself in the world. In the same way that she preferred her father's company as a child, as a teenager, her forays into the world have the effect of sending her further back into the safety of her home; to the familiar comfort of her father: 'Perplexed and unhappy she would seek out her father on all social occasions' (Hall, 82: 77).

Other people, then, bolster Stephen's sense that her security lies not with them but with her home and family. When she does meet people – Angela and Martin – with whom she forms more than superficial attachments, the sign of her commitment to them is wanting to bring them into and make them part of Morton.

Stephen's position in relation to society and nature is presented ominously through the knowing, narrative voice: 'She had not yet learnt her hard lesson – she had not yet learnt that the loneliest place in the world is the no-man's-land of sex' (Hall, 82: 77). It hints of more, and worse, to come. At the same time, the ambiguity returns. Is the reference to sex general, commenting on the difficulties that it brings for everyone? Or is the reference more particular? Are we being asked to see Stephen's status as neither one thing nor the other, – the third sex?

Certainly at this stage in her development, Stephen is aligned with neither men nor women. As she develops, she finds her particular role in relation to each. Where conflict develops between herself and men, as it does with Roger Antrim, Ralph Crossby, and Martin Hallam, it is in the context of rivalry for a woman's affection. In the absence of such conflict, her affinity is with men. Her effect upon women is far more disturbing. Free to dress as she pleases and wear her hair short, her distance from the conventions of femininity is clearly signalled.

When she and Mary become acquainted with Lady Massey, it is Mary who is favoured, and only through her, Stephen. Stephen's impact on other women is most clearly explored through the Comtesse de Mirac, Martin Hallam's aunt. Her reaction echoes back to Mr Antrim's, providing continuity for Stephen as child and woman. These two women

Stephen Gordon and Other People

symbolize the reactions of all married and respectable women – repulsion. Stephen becomes: 'The type that she most mistrusted ... a creature who aping the prerogatives of men had lost all the charm and grace of a woman' (Hall, 82: 422). Lady Massey cannot admit Stephen's inversion, much as earlier Mrs Antrim: 'was never quite clear as to what she suspected, but felt sure it must be something outlandish' (Hall, 82: 89).

The hostility derives from the flaunting of convention and this focuses lesbianism's invisibility. Even when it causes such hostility, it cannot be named. What disturbs is the disruption of sex distinction, a rigid system emphasized at every opportunity, by which Stephen is shown as constantly thwarted or caught unawares. Women, far more than men, oversee this system. Stephen's flouting of it takes her outside the sphere of their influence. Consequently, it is men, rather than women, who throughout the novel act as her guides and supports. The pattern begins with her father, who takes an unusually attentive part in her upbringing, and it continues throughout her life. Towards the novel's end, when Martin re-enters her life, he is shown winning their dog's affection. The dog 'discerning in the man a more perfect thing, a more entirely fulfilling companion' (Hall, 82: 425). For all its bathos, there is an element of truth conveyed. The novel's high evaluation of all things male leaves a strong suggestion that Stephen herself finds the man 'a more perfect thing'. Not perfect as a partner or a love object, but as a role model. Each stage of her development has had a man in attendance, providing support, approval, companionship.

In the early years the role is filled by her father, supplemented by Col Antrim. Although the text emphasizes how insignificant Col Antrim is within his own home, he excels on the hunting field, an arena that has powerful compensatory effects for the young Stephen too. Col Antrim becomes the independent, external voice that confirms Stephen's horse-riding ability, even if it 'amused and surprised him' (Hall, 82: 39). He defends Stephen to others at the hunt who are more grudging in their approval. His support is, however, strictly limited. Within his own home, he has no standing and cannot provide Stephen

30

Stephen Gordon and Other People

with any comfort for her social awkwardness.

The painful shyness and agony of social gatherings are temporarily put into respite by the appearance of Martin Hallam. They meet at the Antrim's New Year party, something Stephen attended only to please her mother. Their mutual oddness is the basis of their friendship. Martin lives in British Columbia and is described as loving trees: 'with a primitive instinct, with a strange and inexplicable devotion' (Hall, 82: 91). He talks about his trees; Stephen is content to listen. The immediacy of their friendship is described approvingly in terms that draw on masculinity: Martin: 'spoke simply, as one man will speak to another' Stephen listens and asks thoughtful questions: 'such as one man will ask of another' (Hall, 82: 91).

The brotherliness of their relationship is stressed and the friendship is rooted in the shared activities of riding and fencing. There is also a spiritual dimension. Martin is described as being: 'A queer, sensitive fellow' (Hall, 82: 92), and it is his own oddness that responds to 'the charm and strangeness of Stephen – her very strangeness it was that allured him' (Hall, 82: 95).

Each of them has known loneliness and thus better appreciates their new companionship. They also have an affinity based on dealing with loneliness through nature and the company of animals.

Inevitably Martin falls in love and asks Stephen to marry him. This eventuality appears never to have occurred to her and she reacts with horror.

> He was saying amazing, incredible things ... she was staring at him in a kind of dumb horror, staring at his eyes that were clouded by desire, while gradually over her colourless face there was spreading an expression of the deepest repulsion – terror and repulsion he saw on her face.
>
> (Hall, 82: 96–7)

Stephen's reaction is extreme to what is, after all, a fairly commonplace assumption, reached by everyone else, except her. It functions both as a dramatic incident within the plot: What will now happen to Stephen? Could her father be right?, and as

31

Stephen Gordon and Other People

an index of how far removed Stephen is from conventional understandings of sexuality.

Important as the private development of their friendship is, of greater significance is the effect once Stephen is seen to conform. Benevolence descends upon them. Commenting to Puddle that she has grown fond of Martin and will miss him when he goes, Puddle: 'Quite suddenly beamed at Stephen and kissed her – Puddle, who never betrayed her emotions' (Hall, 82: 95). At earlier points, when Puddle has suspected Stephen's lesbianism, she has been silenced, unable to convey anything at all. Heterosexuality, on the other hand, is a thing to be acknowledged, spoken about, and rewarded.

Martin is liked and encouraged to visit by both Lady Anna and Sir Philip, fussed over by the one, given the run of the stables by the other. Stephen is still the focus of local gossip, but of a quite different order: 'On the whole they gossiped quite kindly with a great deal of smiling and nodding of heads. After all the girl was just like other girls' (Hall, 82: 95).

Her mother softens: 'Her heart went out in affection to Stephen, as it had not done since the girl was a baby' (Hall, 82: 95), as she plans marriage and grandchildren. She is chided in this planning by Sir Philip, though even he hopes: 'Had he been mistaken? Perhaps after all he had been mistaken' (Hall, 82: 95). His question strikes the only harsh note in this bliss, returning us again to the hints and portents concerning Stephen that pepper the novel. It reads like some kind of suspense story: Will she/won't she? Is she/isn't she?

One of the most important functions this relationship performs is to indicate, tantalizingly briefly, what life could be like for Stephen. In this way, the harshness of life as it has been, and will continue to be after this idyll, is played up. The repercussions, when Martin, hurriedly leaves after being refused by Stephen, are severe: 'They had been so eager to welcome the girl as one of themselves, and now this strange happening – it made them feel foolish which in turn made them angry' (Hall, 82: 106).

Martin's presence transformed Stephen's social standing. Stephen now stands alone, 'an outlaw' while her neighbours

32

Stephen Gordon and Other People

apply themselves to the task of a 'policing nature' (Hall, 82: 108). When he goes, the protection he afforded, a protection that will be mimicked much later by his presence in the Paris she and Mary know, will also disappear.

Seventeen years later, a letter arrives for Stephen. It is from Martin, expressing the hope that their friendship can be resurrected. He is staying in Paris, unaware that Stephen has also made it her home. She is eager to resume their friendship. Although the narrative tell us that Stephen: 'had starved for just this – the friendship of a normal and sympathetic man whose mentality being very much her own, was not only welcome but reassuring' (Hall, 82: 424), what we see is the important role Martin plays in Mary's social life.

His behaviour echoes his salvationary role towards the young Stephen, the acceptable face of heterosexuality. Stephen, after the first visit to his aunt, resolves not to go again, although Mary frequently accompanies Martin there. There is little indication of any depth of feeling between Martin and Stephen. Even when Stephen tells him why she had to leave Morton, his concern is for Mary. 'Martin said nothing for quite a long time, and when he did speak it was very gravely: "Mary – how much does she know of all this?"' (Hall, 82: 427).

Martin's sympathies for her are very reminiscent of her father's. He pities her, regrets her situation, but is ultimately cowardly – and therefore useless to Stephen – in his love. 'Why need this have come upon you – this incomprehensible dispensation? It's enough to make me deny God's existence' (Hall, 82: 427).

Their friendship is driven out by the battle to win Mary's affection and loyalty, Martin's assertions of what Mary needs strike at the very heart of what Stephen wishes she were able to give her: 'She needs all the things that it's not in your power to give her: children, protection, friends whom she can respect and who'll respect her' (Hall, 82: 433). It is Stephen who must prove herself against Martin, insisting that he stays at the two points he wishes to leave. First, when he is unable to contain his feelings for Mary, secondly when he realizes he cannot win her away from Stephen.

Stephen Gordon and Other People

In doing so she engages his 'combative manhood' (Hall, 82: 433) in a fight that evokes Roger Antrim's contemptuous sneer that he doesn't fight with girls:

> I won't consent to your going, Martin. You think that I can't hold the woman I love against you, because you've got an advantage over me and over the whole of my kind. I accept that challenge – I must accept it if I'm to remain at all worthy of Mary.
>
> (Hall, 82: 433)

Stephen will insist on this fight, elevating it to an even higher plane than her 'well-nigh perfect' (Hall, 82: 426) friendship with Martin.

The friendship with Martin ultimately ends in tragedy, but for a short while it gave the young Stephen relief against the pressures of social conformity. At later stages in her life, salvation is also brought by men. It is they who have both the insight into her situation and the confidence to speak to her about it directly. Two of the most significant points in her life; the move to Paris, and her discernment of the hand of God in the creation of all homosexuals; are reached through male guidance. Of these, Brockett, who remains constant in her life, is disparagingly compared to Martin Hallam. He is a gay man, presented as something of a fop. Puddle is extremely wary of him:

> But for such as Stephen, men like Martin Hallam could seldom exist; As friends they would fail her, while she in her turn would fail them as lovers. Then what remained? Jonathen Brockett? Like to like. No, no an intolerable thought!
>
> (Hall, 82: 244)

The basis of their friendship is writing. He is presented as an astute critic as well as a talented playwright. A source of tension in the relationship is that Brockett constantly alludes to Stephen's sexuality; he wants it acknowledged between them. Stephen finds this unbearable, as she does the too obvious signs of his own:

Stephen Gordon and Other People

> He was in his most foolish and tiresome mood – the mood when his white hands made odd little gestures, when his laugh was too high and his movements too small for the size of his broad shouldered, rather gaunt body. Stephen had grown to dread him in this mood.
>
> (Hall, 82: 230)

It is he, however, who has the courage to criticize her latest book; to whom she asks: ' "What must I do to save my work?" for she realised that he had been speaking the stark, bitter truth; that indeed she had needed no one to tell her that her last book had been altogether unworthy' (Hall, 82: 233).

Brockett's advice to her, his assessment of why her writing has gone stale, reminds Stephen of her father's advice, part of the pull to maleness that defines Stephen's life. After he has gone, Puddle attempts to deflect his criticism: 'I didn't agree with one word he said. I expect he's jealous of your work' (Hall, 82: 234). Puddle means well, but Stephen does not need reassurance. Here, at the outset of her career as a writer, Stephen is shown as having outstripped the advice of women. Only men can guide her now. Brockett suggests a complete break with routine, stressing Paris, and this strikes a chord with Stephen's own restlessness and need for change.

Puddle and Stephen go to visit Paris and Stephen, almost on impulse, buys a house there. Brockett is her guide, introducing her to society and sharing his familiarity with the city. He also attempts to make her aware of the city's lesbian traditions:

> Those two would often come here at sunset – can't you imagine it, Stephen? They must often have felt pretty miserable, poor souls; sick to death of the subterfuge and pretences. Don't you ever get tired of that sort of thing? My God, I do!
>
> (Hall, 82: 241)

Stephen resists this attempt at shared knowledge and refuses the camaradarie he offers. It is significant that, just as her father had access to knowledge about her lesbianism; so here it is another man who has the power to acquaint her with historical

35

Stephen Gordon and Other People

and contemporary connections to other lesbians. Puddle clearly knows as much as Brockett, yet she keeps her own counsel: 'something started to hammer in Puddle's brain: "Like to like! Like to like! Like to like!" it hammered' (Hall, 82: 250).

Stephen does settle in Paris and enters into a period of contentment and consolidation: making a home, writing, fencing, renewing her friendship with Mlle Duphot, eschewing the Paris of Valérie Seymour. This calm is shattered only by the outbreak of the war.

Brockett, having acted as the catalyst for Stephen's move to Paris, then fades from her life. His support is not of a daily kind, it comes in at points of crisis, to guide and resolve. In war, which is amongst other things a proving ground for masculinity, Brockett is used to highlight Stephen's dissatisfaction with herself. Brockett enlists emphasizing Stephen's frustration that she cannot. She is scathing about Brockett's: 'foolish gestures, and the high little laugh' (Hall, 82: 270). Her scorn stems from a bitterness that he has a role in the war, can prove himself through it, participating in what Stephen values most highly: courage, patriotism, and service. Brockett may be queer, but at least he's a man.

> Every instinct handed down by the men of her race, every decent instinct of courage, now rose to mock her.... England was calling her men into battle, her women to the bedsides of the wounded and dying, and ... of less use to her country, she was, than Brockett.
>
> (Hall, 82: 271)

Stephen's gloom here is checked not by a man, but by Puddle, who shrewdly prophesies: 'This war may give your sort of woman her chance. I think you may find that they'll need you, Stephen' (Hall, 82: 271).

After the war, Brockett resumes their friendship and, unlike his previous tactless hints and suggestions about Stephen's sexuality, his reaction to Mary's presence is one of respectful silence: 'Never by so much as a word or a look did he once allow it to be inferred that his quick mind had seized on the situation' (Hall, 82: 332-3). He impinges very little on their life after this.

Stephen Gordon and Other People

It is only when Mary's depression and illness force a crisis in her relationship with Stephen that Brockett comes back into focus. He takes control of the situation, daring to speak to Stephen about her love life just as he once dared to speak to her about her writing. Once again, it is a man who names the relationship, who has the knowledge about it:

> Look here, I'm not going to pretend any more. Of course we all know that you two are lovers. You're gradually becoming a kind of legend – all's well lost for love, and that sort of thing.... But Mary's too young to become a legend; and so are you, my dear, for that matter. But you've got your work, whereas Mary's got nothing.
>
> (Hall, 82: 347)

Brockett's sincerity in speaking out is emphasized in the text, as is the degree to which it mirrors Stephen's own thoughts. She finds herself in agreement with him. It is as if only when voiced by a man, do these thoughts become valid and something to act upon. Equally, there is a strong sense of Stephen's relief, the kind of calm that comes with needing, and finding, approval:

> A queer sense of relief at the thought that he knew.... Yes, she actually felt a sense of relief because this man knew of her relations with Mary; because there was no longer any need to behave as if those relations were shameful.
>
> (Hall, 82: 350)

At his suggestion, the acquaintance with Valérie Seymour is renewed. This, really, is his last contribution to the novel. He appears as part of that crowd, but his relationship with Stephen becomes strained. Brockett accompanies them on the journey around the most sordid nightclubs, which culminates with the visit to Alec's. The extent of his detachment from Stephen is shown by his assertion to Valérie that: 'This is life, love, defiance, emancipation' (Hall 82: 391); his enquiry after Stephen's happiness and her rebuff because she: 'hated this inquisitive mood, this mood that would feed upon her emotions' (Hall 82: 391). It is as if Brockett must witness the depths of degradation to which he has encouraged Stephen and

Stephen Gordon and Other People

Mary; as if Stephen must realize how inadequate a guide he has been. He leaves them, sulking because Stephen no longer sees him in the role of guide and protector. His position is taken by Valerie Seymour on the one hand and Adolphe Blanc on the other.

Adolphe Blanc is the final man to inherit the mantle of her father's succour. In Alec's bar, as part of a night out with their Parisian lesbian friends, Stephen refuses to dance with Mary in such sordid surroundings. A man, blocked by the crowd of dancers for a moment before her, claims Stephen as his sister. Her first impulse is to hit out, but that impulse is checked by remembering the fox she saw on the first hunt after her father's death: 'a hapless creature ... hopelessly pursued ... looking for God who made it' (Hall, 82: 394). Stephen Gordon finally admits the claims of 'her kind' and stands with them, to face the harsh and hostile world of other people, her destiny finally reached.

Distressed by what she sees, and overwhelmed by the recognition of what she shares with these men, Stephen is comforted by Adolphe. His behaviour invokes memories of her father: 'He patted her knee as though she were young, very young and in great need of consolation' (Hall, 82: 394). He urges Stephen towards a sense of her own destiny. He recognizes the despair around them, but refuses to see it as the end, only the beginning: 'From their very degradation that spirit will rise up to demand of the world compassion and justice' (Hall, 82: 396). From their previous conversation, about the need for a book to be written, which will: 'make the ignorant think ... bring home the sufferings of millions; only one of ourselves can some day do that.... It will need great courage but it will be done' (Hall 82: 395). We know that Stephen, whose courage has never been in doubt, will answer that course. Indeed, as with her other mentors, she acknowledges: 'This man was actually speaking her thoughts' (Hall, 82: 396).

At this point in the novel what is expected of her from men actually accords with what women, specifically Puddle, have also anticipated for her:

38

Stephen Gordon and Other People

Nothing's completely misplaced or wasted, I'm sure of that – and we're all part of nature. . . . For the sake of all the others who are like you, but less strong and less gifted perhaps, many of them, it's up to you to have the courage to make good.

(Hall, 82: 208)

Adolphe Blanc moves homosexuality, and Stephen's destiny as its advocate, from nature into the hands of God. It is through him that preparation is made for the role that will sustain her once Mary has left. At that stage, all mortal men are behind her, the line of support, guidance, and duty that began with her own father dissolves into the archetypal Christian image of God the Father, before whom she must plead her own and others' right to existence.

Chapter Three

HOW DOES STEPHEN GORDON GET ON WITH OTHER WOMEN?

FEMININITY is very difficult for Stephen Gordon: she cannot internalize what it means to be a woman: how to act and respond: 'All my life I've never felt like a woman' (Hall, 82: 204). The text labours the point. From birth onwards she is seen to look, and want to be, male. One of the most problematic aspects of *The Well of Loneliness* is the extent to which a critique of femininity becomes tangled up with criticisms of women: an inability to differentiate between what patriarchy expects women to be and what they innately are. This is made more difficult because much of Stephen's relation to her own womanhood emerges through the very difficult relationship she has with her own mother.

Our perception of where Stephen stands is also complicated. In her situation, femininity means being for a man. In refusing to comply, Stephen's behaviour is admirable; but problems arise because she cannot really escape from the patriarchy. If she is not 'for a man', then she must be a man; and her behaviour towards women does draw on traditional male values.

MOTHER AND DAUGHTER

The Well of Loneliness is not a mother-blaming book: Stephen's mature relationships with women are never traced back to things her mother did or didn't do. And yet that relationship is fundamental to the novel. The person who

40

Stephen Gordon with Other Women

causes Stephen most pain in the novel is her mother. The world, from whom she must claim homosexuality's rights to exist, first speaks to her in her mother's voice of: 'this unspeakable outrage that you call love' (Hall, 82: 203). It sets the terms of Stephen's crusade: to be able to speak of her own and others' existence, to counter the charge of outrage by asserting homosexuality's place within humanity and divinity, and finally, to establish that it is genuine love, not vice. Lady Anna has caused Stephen pain throughout her life. She is banished from Morton after her mother's tirade against the struggle it has been to mother her:

> All your life I've felt very strangely towards you ... a kind of physical revulsion ... a terrible thing for a mother to feel ... but now I know that my instinct was right; it is you who are unnatural, not I.'
>
> (Hall, 82: 203)

Lady Anna now has, in her terms, an excuse for doing what she has in fact done since birth: reject Stephen. Her rejection is rooted in a lack of understanding, stitching this important theme into the novel early on: 'If she'd only talk to me as she talks to Philip, I might get to understand her' (Hall, 68: 30), muses Anna about the 7-year-old Stephen. The book's pleas for tolerance rests on the charitable idea that homosexuality is simply misunderstood. Here, in a relationship that moves through the novel's entire span, the consequences of misunderstanding are explored in painful, intimate detail.

As a small child, Stephen is given to fits of temper that her mother cannot relieve: 'her eyes would look cold, though her voice might be gentle.... The hand would be making an effort to fondle, and Stephen would be conscious of that effort' (Hall, 82: 11). At this stage there is the will to love, but that is not enough. Anna is conscious of what is going on, prays for guidance about it but never confides her fears to her husband. In fact, she disguises her feelings for him. The only time Anna can feel something other than antagonism is when she erases her daughter's independence, remembering: 'when this creature had clung to her breast, forcing her to love it by its own

41

Stephen Gordon with Other Women

utter weakness' (Hall, 82: 11). The implications of this for Stephen are grim, but so too are they for Anna. Breast-feeding the child, she has a centrality and importance that she never regains. Stephen's upbringing illustrates the damage done by silence, by not trying to speak together. It is, too, a most graphic account of the diminishing of a mother's power and the terrible consequences of this. Although Anna has very little power to determine the course of her daughter's life, she does have a significant impact upon it. Stephen's first awareness of beauty is associated with her mother. She feels something: 'almost amounting to worship, that her mother's face had awakened' (Hall, 82: 11).

As well as recognizing in Anna a beauty she does not possess, Stephen will also pick up the negative response she produces in Anna. There is no pleasure, indeed much anger, contemplating Stephen 'As though the poor, innocent seven-year-old Stephen were in some way a caricature of Sir Philip; a blemished, unworthy, maimed reproduction' (Hall, 82: 11).

Stephen, however, idealizes her mother. She is the first of many women for whom the expression of her love will take the form of protection. There is something disturbing about the 7-year-old Stephen comforting her mother, stroking her hand and making her promise not to worry if Stephen promises to try and control her temper. This protective role rehearses how Stephen behaves with the women she loves passionately as an adult.

For much of her life, Anna acquiesces with Sir Philip. She is, for example, uneasy about calling her Stephen, but Sir Philip's stubbornness holds sway. The only time Anna directly challenges him, she is defeated. After Stephen's fight with Roger Antrim, Anna tackles Sir Philip. Stephen returns inconsolable and resisting her mother's comfort; a comfort not offered by her father. When she has been put to bed, Anna voices her worry that his experimental childrearing isn't working. Lady Anna pinpoints it as not good for Stephen and not good for her. Sir Philip will only modify his plan, agreeing to a governess but stressing Stephen's need for a fine education. He will neither admit the truth of what Anna says nor explain

Stephen Gordon with Other Women

to her why he believes his actions are necessary: 'His own conviction that her child was not as other children' (Hall, 82: 51).

There is, in one sense, no contest: 'A look that she knew well had come into his eyes, a cold, resolute expression' (Hall, 82: 51). Anna is vulnerable because of her own lack of education, made to feel she has no rights over her own child. When she says: 'I don't understand, why shouldn't you trust *me*, Philip?' (Hall, 82: 51), he is evasive. He does not answer her question about trust. Instead, he focuses on understanding: 'There's nothing for you to understand' (Hall, 82: 51), he lies.

The fury Anna later feels and directs towards Stephen; the fury at learning that there was, in fact, much to understand, belongs partly to her husband. Whatever Anna may actually feel about the fact of her daughter's homosexuality, much of her rage must stem from his deception. Here is yet another exclusion, something else shared only by Stephen and her father.

As Stephen grows up, Anna is in retreat from her daughter and in despair. There are skirmishes over how Stephen is to dress, how she is to conduct herself socially, but they are desultory contests. Anna, acutely aware of how little she matters, turns bitter. Unable to love her daughter, she:

> Would sometimes hear herself speaking to Stephen in a way that would make her feel secretly ashamed ... covertly, cleverly gibing, with such skill that the girl would look up at her bewildered ... she would laugh it off lightly, as though all the time she had only been jesting, and Stephen would laugh too, a big, friendly laugh. But Sir Philip would not laugh, and his eyes would seek Anna's questioning, amazed, incredulous and angry.
>
> (Hall, 82: 79)

The struggle drives a wedge into her relationship with Sir Philip. The crisis comes just after Martin leaves. Again, there is the sense that Anna's extreme reaction, her insistent cruel probing of Stephen, stems from her own feelings of exclusion. Stephen has spoken to Sir Philip, not to her. She had gone to the study, the place that for Anna symbolizes knowledge that

Stephen Gordon with Other Women

both fascinates and is not wanted. On other occasions, Anna, woken by Sir Philip's absence from bed, goes to his study, listens to him pacing up and down, yet cannot connect with him: 'She dared not ask him, she dared not so much as turn the door handle, a haunting premonition of disaster would make her creep away with her question unasked' (Hall, 82: 80). At these times, Anna, goes in and looks at the sleeping Stephen, trying to cope with her resentment by remembering her as a baby: 'memories drawn from this stranger's beginnings' (Hall, 82: 81).

The incident with Martin is a watershed in all sorts of ways. Although Sir Philip has withheld his suspicions, he is brutally frank about the fact that Stephen will not, indeed must not, marry. When Anna protests, sensing something has been held back, she loses control, voicing the fears that have plagued her for years: 'You care nothing for me anymore – you and Stephen are enleagued against me.... She's taken you from me' (Hall, 82: 110) The response is damning and blames Anna: 'If you hate her you've got to hate me; she's my child, I won't let her face your hatred alone' (Hall, 82: 110).

It is impossible, during these quarrels, for Stephen not to know that she is their source and things remain sour until, on Sir Philip's death bed, they forgive each other: 'Rekindled the beacon for their child in the shadow of the valley of death' (Hall, 82: 116).

The circumstances of her father's death, trying to clear snow from Anna's favourite tree, pulls back the distance between them. It has become impossible for Sir Philip to speak to either Anna or Stephen, so the only resolution to that particular stalemate is to heighten the drama. By dying, the ground is cleared for Anna and he to restate their commitment to each other; for Stephen to feel both excluded from but sustained by their love. In this way, Stephen's valorization of her parents' marriage does not require adjustment. It remains her model of an ideal relationship, one in which she finds her place by indentifying with her father.

This goes back to when she was quite young, times when Sir Philip: 'and Anna must get talking, amusing themselves

Stephen Gordon with Other Women

irrespective of Stephen, inventing absurd little games, like two children, which games did not always include the real child' (Hall, 82: 32). The effect upon Stephen is: 'longings for something that she wanted yet could not define – a something that would make her as happy as they were' (Hall, 82: 33).

As she develops, beginning to define her needs, the idealization of this particular marriage grows more explicit. Other people's marriages, especially that of Violet Antrim, produce a most acute sense of exclusion in Stephen; the crisis in her parent's marriage, even before she realizes her part in it, causes her terrible anxiety: 'She would sit and stare at them – these poor, stricken lovers – with eyes that were scared and deeply reproachful: 'You must not let anything spoil your loving, I need it . . . the one perfect thing about me' (Hall, 82: 82).

In trying to describe her feelings for Angela Crossby, Stephen can only do so in the terms of her parent's marriage: 'As my father loves you, I loved. . . . If I could have I'd have married her and brought her home' (Hall, 82: 204–5. Equally, she can only appreciate the enormous disadvantages their relationship labours under at the point where Angela, in too deep, quickly finds her way out by asking Stephen if she could marry her. Her later relationship with Mary settles into a pattern that apes a heterosexual marriage to the point of caricature. It is difficult, in the light of the damage done to Mary's self-esteem by the relationship, to know whether Radclyffe Hall really does advocate marriage as a model for lesbian relationships or not.

Within the novel, her parents' marriage is the only positive example we are given. The Antrim's marriage is presented unfavourably, as something that thwarts and diminishes Colonel Antrim, standing between how he must live and how he would choose to. Violet Antrim's marriage is firmly located in the sphere of property; the Comtesse de Mirac is shown as patiently enduring her husband for the sake of money. This is, aside from Jean and Adèle, Stephen's servants in Paris, no demonstration of the value of marriage to men or to women. Even allowing for some hostility between Stephen and Ralph Crossby, his marriage to Angela provides one of the most

Stephen Gordon with Other Women

graphic illustrations of marriage as a social and economic necessity. It also affords a damning description of married love: 'He was always insistent when most ineffectual.... He climbed into bed with the sly expression that Angela hated – it was so pornographic.... After which followed one or two flaccid embraces, together with much arrogant masculine bragging' (Hall, 82: 151–6). Heterosexuality appears throughout in a very jaded light.

Djuna Barnes was part of the lesbian circle grouped around Natalie Barney in Paris in the early twentieth century. Radclyffe Hall and Una Troubridge were friendly with them and appear in the satire Barnes wrote about the set, *The Ladies Almanack*. The Almanack concerns the life and times of Dame Evangeline Mussett:

> Who was in her heart one grand Red Cross for the Pursuance, the Relief and the Distraction of such Girls as in their Hinder Parts and their Fore Parts, and in whatsoever Parts did suffer them most, lament cruelly, be it itch of Palm, or quarters most horribly burning.
>
> (Barnes, 1928: 6)

Evangeline's father bears a striking resemblance to Sir Philip:

> her father, be it known, spent many a windy Eve pacing his library in the most normal of Night-Shirts, trying to think of ways to bring his erring Child back into that Religion and Activity, which has ever been thought sufficient for a woman.
>
> (Barnes, 1928: 8)

Djuna Barnes mocks Hall's commitment to marriage, but does so stressing the symmetry of a supposed marriage between women, rather than emphasizing separate roles for each. Whether this is Djuna Barnes' gentle mocking of Hall's actual ideas about sex-role difference or not is hard to say.

> Among such Dames of which we write, were two British Women. One was called Lady Buck and Ball, and the other plain Tilly-Tweed-in-Blood. Lady Buck and Ball sported a monocle and believed in spirits, Tilly-Tweed-in-Blood sported a stetson and believed in Marriage. They came to the temple of the Good

Stephen Gordon with Other Women

Dame Musset, and they sat to Tea, and this is what they said: 'Just because Woman falls, in this Age, to Woman, does that mean we are not to recognise Morals? What has England done to legalise these Passions? Nothing! Should she not be brought to Task that never once through her gloomy weather have two Dear Doves been seen approaching in their Bridal laces to pace, in Stately Splendour, up the Altar Aisle, there to be united in Similarity, under Mutual Vows of Loving, Honouring and Obeying, while the One and the Other fumble in that nice Temerity, for the equal gold Bands, that shall make of one a Wife, and the other a Bride?

Most wretchedly never that I have heard of, nor one such pair seen later in a Bed of Matrimony, tied up in their best Ribands, all under a Canopy of Cambric, Bosom to Bosom, Braid to Braid, Womb to Womb!'

(Barnes, 1928: 18–19)

Stephen's idealization of her parents' marriage causes difficulties because it is her father whom she most admires and imitates. A tension arises because her mother comes to represent all that she most aspires to, in terms of the appreciation of female beauty; and that which she spurns. Over time, the emphasis shifts; by the end of the book, Stephen is much clearer and much more detached about her mother and in many ways much less idealistic than she was at its outset. That the relationship changes is important.

Its importance lies in the extent to which the possibility for change stands against the fixed, predestined character of Stephen Gordon. A predestination that finds a linguistic echo in the density of 'musts' within the book. Stephen, and others, are shown as compelled, driven to behave and think in certain ways. This is closely allied to the deterministic view of sexuality, specifically homosexuality, in the novel. It is important, given the argument for tolerance being made, that the homosexual is seen to have no choice. It is irresistible, imposed upon them. At the same time, however, the attitudes of people more generally must be shown as capable of change.

Although there are no instances documented in the novel of hostility transformed by knowledge and understanding into acceptance, that potential is confirmed by the more general dynamics of change at work in all the relationships. The novel

Stephen Gordon with Other Women

stresses constancy as a virtue: in Stephen's memory of her father; in Puddle's service; in responsibility to Mlle Duphot; in Martin Hallam's recognition of the mutually important friendship he shared with Stephen. But, adherence to that virtue is not elevated above other considerations. Stephen wrestles with the implications of her father's silence; the question of whether Puddle will accompany Stephen away from Morton is genuine, as is her struggle to accept that during and after the war her place is no longer with Stephen but with Lady Anna; Stephen is allowed to forget Collins. The effect is to demonstrate that relationships between people are influenced by a number of factors that are not fixed.

The most spectacular example is the relationship between Mary and Stephen, which is shown to have an internal logic as well as being susceptible to things external to it. The nature and consequences of those changes, in terms of Stephen driving Mary into the arms of Martin, arms that she herself arranged to be there, pose tremendous difficulties. However, in this light it is important to register that the inevitability is revealed as having been highly manipulated. It had potential to be different: only after Stephen has won the argument does she arrange her defeat.

The relationship that undergoes the most profound transformation is that between Stephen and her mother. This is hardly surprising, given how fraught the relationship is from the outset and the important role it takes between women generally, in determining questions of identity, self-esteem, and independence. Issues of power are never very far away, and all the more naked here as they operate between two women who, as widow and daughter, have substantial financial independence from each other. The ties that bind are a mixture of the emotional and the social. What is significant about this relationship, both for Stephen Gordon's character and a more general profile on mothering, is that it is never passive. Anna and Stephen struggle equally, if unsuccessfully, with its difficulties.

As a young child, Stephen takes after her father. She has his looks, develops his interests, and sees him as a model. She is not

Stephen Gordon with Other Women

like her mother, does not imitate nor model herself upon her. In this way, from an early age, she is awkwardly caught between the sexes: women who, recognizing the freedom and power they have, and ally themselves with men, do so at the risk of alienating women who feel this to be an implied or actual criticism of themselves. The alienation from her mother is repeated in Stephen's dealing with other older women; they are at worst suspicious and hostile, at best, reserved.

Stephen has a complicated relationship to her mother; very conscious of her beauty yet unable to love her. The sense of difference Stephen feels about herself is both indexed against her mother and removes her from her. This is made explicit at the point where Sir Philip realizes the truth about his daughter, a truth he withholds from both Anna and Stephen.

> Anna, so perfect a thing, so completely reassuring; and then that indefinable quality in Stephen that made her look wrong in the clothes she was wearing, as though she and they had no right to each other, but above all no right to Anna.
>
> (Hall, 82: 23)

Anna's struggles to love her child reach a crisis during adolescence, where Sir Philip's interest in Stephen's writing and overall intellectual development powerfully excludes her. She feels abandoned by both her husband and her child and this is projected onto the issue of dress. Stephen and Anna fight bitterly about clothes: it is her last attempt to claim something of her daughter for herself. Sir Philip has actively encouraged Stephen to turn to him: 'Don't worry your mother, just come to me, Stephen' (Hall, 82: 25), he tells her, after the incident with Collins, setting a pattern that is broken only by his death, too late for Anna and Stephen to repair the damage.

At the height of her misery about Angela, Stephen longs to be able to confide in and be comforted by her mother; recognizing the immense, unconditional love between mothers and daughters as something she does not have. The impulse is described as being preposterous; Stephen experiences herself as 'shamelessly childish' (Hall, 82: 162). This both underlines the

49

Stephen Gordon with Other Women

absence of sympathy between them and hints at the impossibility of mature relationships between mothers and daughters.

Stephen recognizes the differences between her feelings for her mother and father early on, and increasingly her regard and affection for her mother are present only for the sake of her father or his memory. They go on trying until the incident with Angela Crossby. Puddle's commentary on this condemns Anna's behaviour well before the crisis that leads to Stephen leaving Morton. This is partly a device to illustrate that Stephen cannot rely on her mother's support and understanding, while anticipating the hostile reaction likely if she was ever to learn the truth about Stephen. It is Puddle's grasp of that hostility that prevents her from speaking more openly to Stephen herself. She is proved to have anticipated correctly: Anna poses Stephen the choice of one of them leaving Morton, knowing full well that Stephen will go.

Stephen's departure for Paris some years later is the occasion for a very frank letter to her mother, which reflects some of Stephen's changed thinking about her. Now that she is more confident about who she is, Stephen is able to measure herself against her mother in terms other than her own lack. There is a degree of scorn for her mother's life that bolsters Stephen's courage: 'Her mother's protected life that had never had to face this terrible freedom. Like a vine that clings to a warm southern wall it had clung to her father – it still clung to Morton' (Hall, 82: 236).

It is a positive stage in Stephen's development to assert her sexual identity and get so angry with her mother, not simply because she is her mother, but because through her, the most sustained and damaging versions of lesbian identity are carried in the novel. Stephen envies her mother the ease of her loving and its social endorsement, and is angered by the harshness shown to her:

> What right had a mother to abominate the child that had sprung from her own secret moments of passion ... a hard and pitiless woman this mother must be for all her soft beauty; shamelessly finding shame in her off-spring.
>
> (Hall, 82: 236)

Stephen Gordon with Other Women

Stephen writes to her mother telling her that she is leaving the country and has no wish to see her again. The letter is written, then read three times, nothing is added or taken away. Three is a magic number; the number of fairy tales and here it confirms the irrevocable break with the past.

Her letter asserts the primacy of her work and the recognition that, as it needs to be protected and nurtured, she must avoid anything that undermines it. She rebels against her mother's definition of her unworthiness, making it clear that she is her parents' daughter: refusing to deny the responsibility her mother has for her at the same time as she emphasizes the differences between her parents' reactions to her: 'If my father had lived he would have shown pity, whereas you showed me none, and yet you were my mother. In my hour of great need you utterly failed me' (Hall, 82: 238). The implication here is that the mother's rejection is the more damaging and hurtful than her father's would have been. This incident ends with a peculiar summary: 'Thus was Anna Gordon baptised through her child as by fire; unto the loss of their mutual salvation' (Hall, 82: 238). The difficulty is partly dredging the meaning out of an overly complicated, biblical sentence. It seems to be saying that the mother's inability to accept her daughter's sexuality, to accept her daughter, makes it the worse for both of them. The family is once more perceived as a potential source of support and stability; its loss is a powerful loss for Stephen,

Throughout the rest of the novel, Stephen returns to Morton only three times. The first occasion is during the war, just before she is posted overseas as an ambulance driver. Whilst there, she dwells less on her banishment than on her father and his death, realizing that: 'Memory – they're the one perfect thing about me' (Hall, 82: 251).

The visit is strained but on her return to London Stephen insists that Puddle must go and live with Anna:

> Puddles' sudden and almost fierce rebellion ... strange to hear such words as these on the kind lips of Puddle. 'I know, I know but she's terribly alone, and I can't forget that my father loved her.' A long silence.
>
> (Hall, 82: 281)

Stephen Gordon with Other Women

Her second visit comes immediately after the war; an opportunity for Puddle to realize the implications of Stephen's relationship with Mary and for her mother to ignore it. The third visit, some months later, is one that does not include Mary in the invitation. Mary, in fact, is never mentioned in her mother's letters.

After this, there are no more visits, no more connections with Morton, mother, or home. Stephen creates her life anew, in Paris, with a new family of servants and friends.

WOMEN AS LOVERS

Stephen falls in love three times during the novel. Each of the women – Collins, Angela Crossby, and Mary Llewellyn – are very different from each other, yet there are, from Stephen's point of view, certain consistencies. With each, Stephen's perceptions of what is happening is highly romantic. It is not simply a matter of emotional delusions; even with Collins and Angela her attraction is acknowledged and played up to. Stephen does not invent or imagine the interactions between herself and other women. What is difficult is the meaning she and others, including the women involved, ascribe to it.

The romance element is one way of locating what is happening for Stephen in a structure of feeling and behaviour known to her and to the reader. It makes it comprehensible because everyone can recognize the conventions. At the same time, though, being a woman undoes that work of normalization, rendering lesbianism strange and Stephen even stranger. Collins, Angela, and Mary all act and respond within the conventions of romance: it is Stephen who stands outside of them. The novel stresses this at the expense of making the point that either of the two women who choose each other, rather than men, transgress the conventions of social and sexual conduct.

A more significant characteristic of the three relationships is the inequality structured into them. Collins is a servant, Angela is financially dependent on a man, and Mary has no

52

Stephen Gordon with Other Women

independent financial means. None of the three women are in any way socially equal to Stephen. They become less negative than they could be, as examples of lesbian love, because we see no evidence of an equal, reciprocal love.

With Mary, where the love is reciprocated, there is no equality. This is partly because of the nature of their social roles, showing once again how socially determined are the sexual and emotional options available to lesbians. Love is shown to be incapable of conquering all, yet even up to the moment of separation, it is presented, between Stephen and Mary, as if it ought to be. It is interesting that although the authorial text and Stephen's own motivation in rejecting Mary are weighted towards the social expectations and options for her as a normal, heterosexual woman: raising children, being accepted in society, etc., the act that drives her from Stephen is the betrayal of that love. It is only at the point where Mary believes Stephen to have been unfaithful to her with Valerie Seymour that her commitment is shaken.

The inequalities in their relationship arise partly because they do not work. They do not have the public occupation and validation of themselves, or an arena where Mary's skills could balance and become equivalent to the privilege of birth and wealth that Stephen has. Restricted to the private sphere, the inequalities are highlighted. Although Stephen perceives Mary as vulnerable, the text makes it clear that she has considerable strength. She is first introduced to us as an orphan: a role that suggests a certain vulnerability but can also, as it does here, provide her with an enormous freedom from the constraints of family expectation and control. Mary, we are told: 'was neither so frail nor so timid as Mrs Breakspeare had thought her' (Hall, 82: 287).

But the absence of paid work in peacetime does create a huge gulf between them. Stephen's model for a partnership is that of her parent's marriage, yet she is unable to reproduce any of that in her relationship with Mary. There is no network of social obligation and custom to provide a focus for activity: there is nothing that bolsters self-identity. The work of caring for a loved one and a home is superfluous: Stephen has had years of

Stephen Gordon with Other Women

making a home for herself and there is nothing for Mary to do:

> Mary rolled up the stockings with a sigh of regret; alas, they would not require darning. She was at the stage of being in love when she longed to do womanly tasks for Stephen. But all Stephen's clothes were discouragingly neat; Mary thought that she must be very well served, which was true – she was served, as are certain men, with a great deal of nicety and care by the servants.
>
> (Hall, 82: 325)

Mary thus lacks a role within the private sphere – nurturing Stephen; she lacks a social role, certainly as a lesbian, but more so simply as a single woman and, unlike Stephen who has her writing, she has no absorbing occupation, nothing to extend herself through except her connection to Stephen.

Although the progress of each affair has certain similarities, not least that they end unhappily, the women involved are each very different. Generally, the book is pervaded by a theory of sexuality that does not acknowledge the possibility of lesbians being attracted to other lesbians. It is a perverse theory of lesbianism, but nevertheless one that had considerable credibility at the time Radclyffe Hall was writing. Through the three women she loves, we are able to explore what kind of women are drawn towards lesbianism. Each of the three represents progression for Stephen, which again adds importantly to the theme of change. Few people in this book are doomed to the endless repetitions of behaviour: change is shown to be both possible and desirable for all.

In considering them, Collins presents us with a problem. Her story is central to the book as the consequences for Stephen are far-reaching. As the first example of her attraction to a woman it is also highly charged. However, the plausibility of the whole affair is stretched because it happens with Stephen is 7 years old. In order to make sense of what happens between Stephen and Collins, it is necessary to suspend the knowledge that she is 7 years old and concentrate on it as an example of first love, which it clearly seeks to be. Why Radclyffe Hall should have made these events take place at such a tender age is not clear. Perhaps it is a

Stephen Gordon with Other Women

way of underlining how innate the lesbian impulse is in Stephen; or perhaps it is the only way to fit everything in.

The attraction Stephen has for Collins is presented in terms of romance: much of what happens, happens in the imagination. Stephen's world is heightened. Dizzy with the infatuation of a look, a smile, a kiss, she finds her usual routines and pleasures disturbed. This is to be the case with each of her lovers: they put life into relief, make it impossible to go back to. For the young Stephen, what she gets from her infatuation with Collins far outweighs what she gives. Collins is the least realized of all Stephen's women, and where she is characterized, it is extremely unflattering.

By presenting Collins as a slovenly slow-witted, deceitful girl, Hall is both maintaining popular prejudice against servants and demonstrating how deeply the attraction lies for Stephen. It is natural to her: she is not led astray or seduced by an older, sexually sophisticated woman. The moment of realizing attraction is all down to Stephen:

> Collins looked up and suddenly smiled, then all in a moment Stephen knew that she loved her – a staggering revelation! Collins said politely: 'Good morning, Miss Stephen. 'She had always said 'Good morning, Miss Stephen' but on this occasion it sounded alluring – so alluring that Stephen wanted to touch her, and extending a rather uncertain hand she started to stroke her sleeve.
>
> (Hall, 82: 13)

Although Collins in no way exploits Stephen sexually, she does take advantage of her infatuation. An incident develops between Collins and the nurse in which she lies. This becomes pivotal for Stephen. It is all highly melodramatic and turns on Stephen's utter inability to understand the nature of life for Collins. This is found again with Angela and Mary, though with each of them there is more awareness and less selfishness. As a very junior servant, Collins is clearly in an awkward position, being seen to interfere in a higher servant's concerns. Likewise her impatience with Stephen; telling her not to get under her feet, produces an exaggerated effect: 'Stephen must

Stephen Gordon with Other Women

slink upstairs thoroughly deflated, strangely unhappy and exceedingly humble' (Hall, 82: 16), which takes no account of the fact that Collins must work. These incidents, however, fuel the rather masochistic notion of love that characterize Stephen's infatuation:

> yet this very injustice seemed to draw her to Collins, since despising, she could still love her ... it was really rather fine to be suffering – it certainly seemed to bring Collins much nearer; it seemed to make Stephen feel that she owned her by right of this diligent pain.
>
> (Hall, 82: 14–19)

Up to this point Collins is presented as weak and irresponsible in that, while she does not encourage Stephen, she does not firmly discourage her either. Our attention is much more focused on Stephen and what she makes of her new feelings, how she responds to them. For Stephen, the main effect is to open a vein of extravagant play acting and exhibitionism. She is displaying herself for and to her loved one, something she does in a more muted way with Angela, something that by the time she meets Mary, is completely crushed out of her.

Here, the form it takes is to dress up as her hero – Young Nelson. Stephen first articulates her wish to be a boy in the context of her attraction to Collins. It is a complex desire, sometimes terribly innocent, as when she asks her father if she could become a man by hard praying or thought. At other times, though, it is simply the laying bare of the agonized relation to femininity that Stephen is to spend most of her life trying to accommodate. She dresses as a boy to please herself and to impress Collins; rebuffed she sinks into: 'feeling all wrong, because she so longed to be someone quite real, instead of just Stephen pretending to be Nelson' (Hall, 82: 17).

The motif that Stephen is out of step with herself as a girl is established early on and clearly tied in to an expression of her sexuality. The anger this entails is directed towards her dolls, symbols of a passive and decorative femininity: ' "I hate you! I hate you!" she would mutter, thumping their innocuous faces' (Hall, 82: 17). Stephen cannot simply ignore the dolls: there is

Stephen Gordon with Other Women

more at stake than something she doesn't like and doesn't want to play with. They are not irrelevant to her and, as the focus of her anger, hint at self-hatred.

At an early age love becomes equated with suffering for Stephen. Her elaborate attempt to acquire a housemaid's knee and thus bear Collins suffering for her, ridiculous as it is, nevertheless has the effect of changing Collins' feelings for her: 'She could not but feel a new interest in the child whom she and the cook had now labelled as "queer", and Stephen basked in much surreptitous petting' (Hall, 82: 20). For all her indulgence of Stephen, Collins does still rebuke her, 'Don't be silly, Miss Stephen' (Hall, 82: 21), is her response to a declaration of love. Stephen discovers Collins in a potting shed with a footman and throws a plant pot, striking and cutting him. Collins is dismissed.

It is Stephen's father rather than her mother who deals with this whole episode, and who is shown to have understood the full implications. During this affair, Sir Philip first takes to spending hours in his study, making fine pencil notes in the margins of von Krafft-Ebbing's *Psychopathia Sexualis*. Sir Philip is firm with Stephen, speaks overtly about her bravery, about how he will now treat her like a boy. Lady Anna is more attentive to Stephen too, is described as 'More diligently fondling Stephen' (Hall, 82: 28) as if she understands the incident with Collins as a search for maternal love and protection, not grasping its sexual connotations.

It is through Collins that Stephen's differences are first clearly articulated in the novel. The feelings Stephen has are not, in themselves, a source of distress to her: that arises from frustration at their lack of reciprocity and the loss of Collins. Collins' importance lies in her catalysing effect. In the midst of the affair, during Spring, Stephen is struggling with her sexual maturation, something she identifies as 'All part of Collins, yet somehow quite different' (Hall, 82: 20). With Collins' departure, Stephen acquires her first pony, whom she solemnly names after her. Just as Stephen outgrows, though never abandons, Collins the pony, once the fine and vigorous Raftery arrives, so too does Stephen outgrow this debilitating, highly

Stephen Gordon with Other Women

emotional, idealized love. She retains and refines in her love for Angela and Mary elements from this affair, but she progresses beyond its more childish excesses.

Through Collins, Stephen and her father become aware of her sexual nature. With Angela Crossby, Stephen learns the consequences of her difference: the implications it has for herself and her relationships with women. The whole of Book Two is devoted to Stephen's affair with Angela. Whereas Collins is presented as well-meaning, if gullible, Angela is treated harshly. She is not Stephen's social equal, having married 'new' money and the initial awkwardness concerning her presence at Morton is as much to do with that as any suspicions concerning the sexual nature of her friendship with Stephen. Puddle herself frustrates her attempt to act as counsel and confidante to Stephen, by misjudging Stephen's first reactions to Angela: 'She's pretty impossible, isn't she, Stephen? ... I suppose you were obliged to give her a lift, but be careful, I believe she's fearfully pushing' (Hall, 82: 132).

As their friendship progresses, it becomes plain that Angela manipulates Stephen for her own ends. Amusing herself with Stephen's sexual and emotional attentions, she ultimately makes her cover and scapegoat for her heterosexual affair with Stephen's old childhood rival, Roger Antrim. The theories of lesbianism that prevailed during the 1920s were concerned to typify lesbians. Within their terms, Angela represents the 'viciousness of acquired homosexuality'. In this way she is neither a true invert, who could not help but be attracted to real women; nor was she herself a real woman who inadvertently and against her nature, falls in love with a true invert. Angela knowingly exploits lesbianism when it suits her to do so.

From Stephen's perspective, however, this damning account of Angela's scheming and cynical behaviour is masked. Despite the damage to Stephen, this affair is much of the time presented in glowing terms. It is good for Stephen, despite the difficulties and problems. Problems that are always perceived by Stephen as less about Angela herself than pressures from outside the relationship. Stephen learns from and grows through each of these situations, adapting and transcending them. Within the

Stephen Gordon with Other Women

novel, they become important in shaping her character. The nobility, strength, and courage that are her hallmarks are forged in the fire of this first, difficult affair.

Angela comes onto the scene at one of Stephen's lowest ebbs. The initial shock of her father's death coming so closely after the disastrous episode with Martin Hallam has begun to recede. But all the plans to go to Oxford and become a writer have disintegrated, Stephen is staying at home with her mother. She is bored, directionless and restless, despite being, at the age of 21, a rich and financially independent woman.

They meet when Stephen breaks up a dog fight. It provides her with a splendid opportunity for masterful gallantry: she separates the dogs, sees to Angela's injury, sees to the dog's wound, and takes both of them home. The exchange between them is flirtatious on Angela's part; embarrassed on Stephen's, aware as she is of her attraction to Angela: 'Then it dawned on the girl that this woman was lovely – she was like some queer flower that had grown up in darkness. Like some rare, pale flower without blemish or stain' (Hall, 82: 130). Angela claims to have been longing to meet Stephen, 'And she stared rather disconcertingly at Stephen, then smiled as though something she saw had amused her' (Hall, 82: 130).

Anticipating the visit to tea, we are shown a Stephen newly aware of pleasure: in the natural world and in herself. She exhibits a vanity about appearance that although not typically feminine, in its concern with tailored suits and neckties, nevertheless highlights the importance of dressing for her. *The Well of Loneliness* here reflects the particular symbolism clothes have within lesbian culture. They differentiate lesbians from heterosexual women, but also mark distinctions between lesbians. J. R. Roberts, *Sinister Wisdom* 9, Spring 1979, gives a fascinating account of the shifts in meaning of the word 'dyke'. She argues that a possible root lies in Old English as 'dight', meaning 'to dress, clothe; to adorn, deck oneself'. She traces a shift from the neutral descriptive terms of dike as 'the full set of male clothing' or 'a man in full dress', to one where it is an abusive term, used against women whose rebellion against male-defined roles often involved or demanded a degree of

Stephen Gordon with Other Women

passing for a male, achieved through dress. Wearing male dress can often be the first expression of lesbian identity and desire: a means of indicating interest and belonging.

Clothes have always been of major significance for Stephen: one sign of her independence and maturity is that she no longer struggles with her mother over what to wear. Stephen dresses to please and display herself much as years before she swaggered before Collins in the garb of young Nelson. At the age of 21, Stephen is closing the identity gap. Previously, the clothes turned into a disappointment, emphasizing the distance between what Stephen was and wanted to be. Now, her clothes express and complement the person she is.

The initial stages of their friendship are presented indulgently. The first visit to Angela is a comic scene: the one self-consciously clumsy, the other wryly amused against a background of warbling birds and convalescent dogs.

> She forgot to inquire about Angela's dog-bite, though the bandaged hand was placed on a cushion; and she also forgot to adjust her new necktie, which in her emotion had slipped slightly crooked. A thousand times in the last few days had she carefully rehearsed this scheme of their meeting, making up long and elaborate speeches; assuming, in her mind, many dignified poses; and yet there she sat on the edge of a chair as though it were the Prickly Cradle.
>
> (Hall, 82: 137)

Reflecting on this first visit, Angela is aware of finding Stephen attractive, but it is of a very different order to Stephen's feelings for her.

> Angela had no need of her hints, not now she had come to know Stephen Gordon. And because she was idle, discontented and bored, and certainly not over-burdened with virtue, she must let her thoughts dwell unduly on this girl, while her curiosity kept pace with her thoughts.
>
> (Hall, 82: 141)

In the way Collins became the means for Stephen to discover her own nature, Angela becomes the means for Stephen to discover the nature of relationships between women; specific-

Stephen Gordon with Other Women

ally what she wants and needs from them. This consent to the relationship is the most significant thing that Angela gives to Stephen. To be, however imperfectly, a focus and partner. While this has an incredibly destructive aspect, it is positive to the extent that Stephen engages with another person and realizes her own attractiveness. The original impulse, towards friendship, is initiated and maintained by Angela; Stephen would be far too frightened to have done so.

Although Angela is not made particularly welcome at Morton, she is able to visit Stephen there. To share Morton with Angela, with the person she loves, is extremely important: Stephen's declaration of love takes the form of claiming Angela for: 'Morton, all beauty and peace – it drifts like that swan does, on calm, deep water. And all this beauty and peace is for you, because you're a part of Morton' (Hall, 82: 144). Angela is still teasing, treating everything very lightly and not fully acknowledging the emotional significance and intensity this has for Stephen. She moves away from her, then back. It is Angela who takes Stephen's hand, who makes the move towards her: 'A step nearer to Stephen, then another, until their hands were touching.... Then Stephen took Angela into her arms, and she kissed her full on the lips, as a lover' (Hall, 82: 144).

Lesbianism is not explicitly referred to, although it is made clear that Angela knows about it: 'You're altogether different from other people' (Hall, 82: 143), she tells Stephen in a curiously ambiguous compliment. It is referred to later as somehow unreal but alluring: 'That glamorous evening, with its spirit of queer, unearthly adventure, with its urge to strange, unendurable sweetness' (Hall, 82: 144).

Although physically attracted by Angela, there is a strong sense that she is almost an excuse for the real romance, which is of place and history. It is certainly made very clear that however carnal Stephen's initial attraction, the consummation she aspires to is one in which love balances the private needs with more significant public needs for community. To link her desire with Morton in this way keeps Stephen within an essentially conservative frame and by doing so, diminishes

Stephen Gordon with Other Women

attempts to see lesbianism as aberrant or decadent. It becomes a means of conferring respectability on the affair:

> We're both filled with the old peace of Morton, because we love each other so deeply – and because we're perfect, a perfect thing, you and I – not two separate people but one. And our love has lit a great, comforting beacon, so that we need never be afraid of the dark anymore – we can warm ourselves at our love, we can lie down together.
>
> (Hall, 82: 144)

As a description of the actual, or potential relationship between Stephen and Angela, her sentiments are pitifully askew. As a description of what Stephen wants from a relationship, it is wholly accurate. That Angela reciprocates, admitting: 'One mighty impulse, one imperative need, and that need was Stephen' (Hall, 82: 144) is explained as due to the force of Stephen's desire. Angela is thus shown as willing to befriend a woman she knows to be a lesbian, but not consciously choosing sexual involvement. The onus for that rests squarely on Stephen, which maintains a traditional view of sexual behaviour between women, that seduction is its only basis.

Stephen falls in love with Angela, something presented as: 'In accordance with the dictates of her nature' (Hall, 82: 145), something perfectly natural to her. This stage of the affair is heavily commented on by the narrative voice, which establishes both the degree to which Angela is unworthy of her love and the immense capacity to love that Stephen possesses:

> This is a hard and sad truth for the telling; those whom nature has sacrificed to her ends – her mysterious ends that often lie hidden – are sometimes endowed with a vast will to loving, with an endless capacity for suffering also, which must go hand in hand with their love.
>
> (Hall, 82: 145)

Stephen dwells on the pleasures and enrichment of the affair, but there is another emphasis within the text from the narrator, which undermines that contentment by describing their kisses as painful and terribly sterile, which distorts Stephen's claim

Stephen Gordon with Other Women

for the naturalness of her love. Angela's role in the affair is shown as culpable and dishonest. She: 'Could never quite let the girl go ... yet the very strangeness of it all was an attraction. Stephen was becoming a kind of strong drug, a kind of anodyne against boredom' (Hall, 82: 146).

Of necessity, a certain amount of deception regarding how and where they spend their time is required. Stephen finds this intolerable, she wants the truth: 'We'll live quite openly together, you and I, which is what we owe to ourselves and our love' (Hall, 82: 148).

Stephen is prepared to give up everything for Angela; Angela won't even consider it. She stalls Stephen before delivering her trump card, asking Stephen if she could marry her. Stephen, acknowledging that she could not, silences them both. Still, at this stage, Stephen's lesbianism is neither known to herself nor named in the text. Angela refers to it as: 'A few rather schoolgirlish kisses. Can I help it if you're – what you obviously are?' (Hall, 82: 148). This indicates how their participation in the affair is weighted in quite different directions, determined by the very different relations to heterosexuality they each have.

For Stephen, loving Angela is simply loving: she will give up her whole world for it. Angela, much as she enjoys Stephen's company and attention, is not willing to threaten her marriage, status, and privilege as a heterosexual woman: 'If you're willing to give up your home, I'm not willing to sacrifice mine.... Ralph's not much of a man, but he's better than nothing' (Hall, 82: 148). It is presented as a foregone conclusion, there is no choice between lesbianism and heterosexuality. It is made perfectly clear here and elsewhere that Angela married for money and that she is very materialistic, yet she rejects Stephen's offer. Stephen is undoubtedly as rich, if not richer than Ralph Crossby, and has more social status. But by home, Angela is also referring to the community of interest within the family and society, against which lesbianism cannot register except as deviance. And families demand the presence of a man, even one as inadequate as Ralph is shown to be. The language used to describe Stephen here is not at all sympathetic: 'A little grotesque in her pitiful passion' (Hall, 82: 149), which seems to

Stephen Gordon with Other Women

function as a way of giving credence to Angela's views. In fact, Stephen herself is one of the strongest proponents of the view that values the stability of home and family, though there is with her, unlike Angela, a struggle to put lesbians into that social structure rather than to adopt heterosexuality.

At this point, Angela and Stephen separate, something that provides an opportunity for lesbianism to be broached in the text. Stephen and Puddle meditate upon it, but do not communicate with each other. Puddle is aware of Stephen's distress but the point is made forcibly that Anna fails, or refused, to notice her distress. We are also given Ralph's views, which are extreme, although he does not register Stephen as any kind of personal threat: 'She's appalling; never saw such a girl in my life ... its enough to make any man see red; that sort of thing wants putting down at birth' (Hall, 82: 150). Unpleasant as these sentiments are, they are countered by two things. The first is that odd and repulsive though Stephen is, she is distinct and known. That she is not alone is an important message in the book and quite contrary to Stephen's perceptions of herself and the overt presentation of her as a unique and isolated creature. Secondly, these opinions come from a man who is presented as an abject human being: tyrannical in his pettiness about food and attention; hyperconscious of wealth and status and emotionally and sexually uninspiring: 'he was also insistent when most ineffectual ... one or two flaccid embraces together with much arrogant masculine bragging' (Hall, 82: 151).

It is at precisely this moment in the text, enduring the flaccid embrace, that Angela is thinking of Stephen. Angela's interest in Stephen is a way of compensating for the awfulness of her man, and as such illustrates both the power of heterosexuality and the positive aspects of lesbianism. One of the myths of lesbianism is that it is a compensatory activity for women who cannot attract men. It is quite daring to show lesbianism, in a very specific sexual context, as a preferred alternative to men. However, any radicalism embodied in Angela Crossby is undermined by her refusal to risk the heterosexual privilege she has. Ultimately she deals with her sexual dissatisfactions within

Stephen Gordon with Other Women

heterosexuality by taking a male lover, and although she is shown as not entirely happy with this, she has no qualms about betraying Stephen, and her own lesbian behaviour, in order to protect her marriage against the possible disclosure of that affair.

The progress of this affair is slow and far from outright in its condemnation of Angela. During this first separation, Stephen suffers a silent anxiety about her identity and her potential to love. She sees love in very chivalrous terms and is aware only of her inability to achieve this: 'She could neither protect nor defend nor honour by loving; her hands were completely empty.... She could only debase what she longed to exalt, defile what she longed to keep pure and untarnished' (Hall, 82: 152).

Because Stephen is so powerless, when the affair with Angela is resumed, it is done so entirely on the latter's terms. These revolve around placating Ralph. The massive inequality between them is asserted, to Angela's advantage. She sets the limits of their relationship and is constantly rebuffing Stephen: she refuses to let her holiday near her, embargoes presents, insists on including Ralph in on some of their time, and so on. Stephen continues to love her, to try and find ways of expressing that love and, in the process, confronts the hostility of the world. She struggles to confide in her mother, but doesn't; runs the gauntlet of shopping for jewellery in Bond Street: 'People stared at the masculine-looking girl who seemed so intent upon feminine adornments. And someone, a man, laughed and nudged his companion: "Look at that! What is it?" ' (Hall, 82: 164). She sends a telegram to Angela when she overstays on a holiday that Violet Antrim hints to Stephen has been enlivened by the friendship between Angela and her brother, Roger.

Upon her return, they spend a passionate evening together during which Angela tells Stephen her life story. For all her deceit and scheming, she articulates a reality about women's relation to men, and the reasons why it is so hard for women to choose each other. Angela wants Stephen to be a man at the same time as she values what is not masculine about her:

Stephen Gordon with Other Women

> She seemed to combine the strength of a man with the gentler and more subtle strength of a woman. And thinking of the crude young animal Roger, with his brusque, rather brutal appeal to the senses, she was filled with a kind of regretful shame.
>
> (Hall, 82: 178)

The reader, but not Stephen, knows the extent of Angela's betrayal and she is described as: 'Longing for the subtle easement of confession, so dear to the soul of woman' (Hall, 82: 178), with the implication that Stephen does not share this.

The story of Angela's hardships and the salvation marriage represents, is presented as making inevitable Angela's priorization of her marriage:

> You're a woman so he couldn't divorce me – I expect that's really what makes him so angry. . . . I couldn't have faced the public scandal that Ralph would have made . . . what Ralph lacks in virility, he tries to make up for by being revengeful.
>
> (Hall, 82: 181)

The effect of this is to increase Stephen's compassion and love for her, something that the authorial voice claims is both Stephen's folly and her redeeming glory.

Ralph's anger at the continuation of their affair finds a palliative only when the triangle between Stephen, Roger, and Angela developes more brazenly: 'The two male creatures who hated each other, would be shamefully united in the bond of their deeper hatred of Stephen' (Hall, 82: 185).

Stephen's love increases under the pressure of Angela's involvement with Roger; it becomes spiritual, a need to care for and protect her. At the same time, their physical love anticipates their separation, driving them to a crisis:

> There would be something crude, almost cruel in their kisses; a restless, dissatisfied hungry thing – their lips would seem bent on scourging their bodies . . . each would be kissing with a well-nigh intolerable sense of loss, with a passionate knowledge of separation.
>
> (Hall, 82: 191)

The crisis comes when Ralph has to go away. Stephen is not

Stephen Gordon with Other Women

permitted to spend the night with Angela but restless, she goes at dawn, simply to look at her house. She sees Roger Antrim leaving. The full extent of the betrayal, the realization that she has been used to draw the heat away from Roger provokes a fit of madness. Stephen drives for hours until she is exhausted and returns to Morton, into Puddle's care. Stephen writes a pleading letter to Angela, setting out what she is, offers, and wants. Angela's inexcusable action is to show this letter to Ralph.

In her letter, Stephen refers to herself as:

> Some awful mistake – God's mistake – I don't know if there are any more like me, I pray not for their sakes, because it's pure hell. But oh, my dear, whatever I am, I just love you and love you.

> (Hall, 82: 199)

Angela claims to have been trying to reform Stephen, at pains to make clear to Ralph that she is: 'Not a pervert . . . not that sort of degenerate creature' (Hall, 82: 200). His anger is directed less at Angela than at 'Stephen and all her kind' (Hall, 82: 200).

Again, as antagonism and prejudice is being expressed, there is the covert messsage of visibility. Stephen, who hopes there are no more like her, is not as alone as she thinks. There are constant hints about the extent of lesbianism: it is a known thing. When Ralph sends the letter to Lady Anna, the affair is over. With Collins, it was the beloved who was dismissed. This time it is Stephen who must go.

It takes Stephen a long time to get over the affair. There comes a point where she acknowledges that: 'She did not feel love these days when she thought of Angela Crossby – that must mean that her heart had died within her. A gruesome companion to have, a dead heart' (Hall, 82: 235). With that romantic love absent, there is room for the expression of sexual passion; we see how she experiences that body that is in such conflict with her spirit. However distressing and guilt-ridden her expressions of lust are, that they find expression is important.

There were times when she longed intensely to see this woman,

67

Stephen Gordon with Other Women

> to hear her speak, to stretch out her arms and clasp them around
> the woman's body – not gently, not patiently as in the past, but
> roughly, brutally even ... something that lay like a stain on the
> beauty of what had once been love.
>
> (Hall, 82: 235)

In her relationship with Angela, Stephen experiences the limitations of loving women. In the process, she and the reader establish that her attraction to women is a permanent feature of her identity, not a youthful phase. The affair, in all sorts of ways, establishes the pattern of Stephen's life to come: Where will she live? How will she live? How far will she trust others? What is natural and what is social is the main theme explored during this time, as is the question of courage. Stephen develops yet more personal attributes of strength, emotional self-sufficiency, and emotional courage: Angela demonstrates a lack of courage that will be echoed and transformed in the character of Mary Llewellyn, a woman who also has nothing, as did Angela, but takes the risk of loving another woman.

After Angela, Stephen withdraws from romance completely. She concentrates on her writing, establishing through that something to anchor her in the world and ground her identity. Puddle is very aware of how damagingly isolated her life is becoming. 'It appeared like a weakness in Stephen; she divined the bruised humility of spirit that now underlay this desire for isolation, and she did her best to frustrate it' (Hall, 82: 214).

Stephen, too, identifies a lack within herself and therefore her writing: 'Why should I live in this great isolation of spirit and body – why should I, why? ... I shall never be a great writer because of my maimed and insufferable body' (Hall, 82: 217).

There is no sense, however, of how Stephen might change this, other than the rather vague idea that she should mix more. Initially, after the move to Paris, Stephen shuns the company of Valérie Seymour, who offers friendship and social contact with other lesbians. Stephen's reasons for doing so are complicated, she wants to be valued in her own right, for herself, and sees that self-hood as quite separate from her lesbian identity. Because Valérie approves of her lesbianism, Stephen thinks this is all she sees in her. In Paris, Stephen's pull towards the past,

Stephen Gordon with Other Women

the values of tradition and family, assert themselves when she meets up with Mlle Duphot and establishes a life based on her work, her recreation, fencing, and a quiet, familial, social life with Puddle and Mlle Duphot and her sister. This calm is disrupted by war, and it is in the heightened, unnatural world of wartime France that Stephen's final, most perfect, love affair develops.

Stephen is an ambulance driver in an all-woman unit operating in France. Mary is a new recruit, assigned as her second driver. She is younger than Stephen, an orphan, and Stephen protects her. The picture of life in the unit is highly romantic; it serves almost as a backcloth against which Stephen can demonstrate the full attainment of heroic stature. It compares oddly with documentary accounts of women's service in the First World War and is at variance with the novel, *Not So Quiet – Step-Daughters of War* by Helen Smith. The most striking difference is in detailing the horrors of war, not just the injuries that these women must try and deal with, but the tyrannies of commanding officers and the deprivations of army life. Lesbianism is dealt with quite differently in the two books also.

In *Not So Quiet*, it is far more brutally and damagingly encountered than Stephen's commander, Mrs Breakspeare, gently suggesting that she takes her turn with other drivers beside Mary and explaining reasonably: 'Thinking it our duty to discourage anything in the nature of an emotional friendship, such as I fancy Mary Llewellyn is on the verge of feeling for you' (Hall, 82: 291). Although the incident here seems unrealistic in that it is smoothly, almost pleasantly dealt with, it is interesting that lesbianism, although dismissed as insignificant, appears common. It is perceived as an immaturity, what a younger woman will feel for an older, but it is, importantly, public knowledge:

> Such times are apt to breed many emotions which are purely fictitious, purely mushroom growths that spring up in a night and have no roots at all, except in our imaginations ... quite natural of course, a kind of reaction, but not wise.

> (Hall, 82: 291)

Stephen Gordon with Other Women

The initial attraction between Stephen and Mary is not romantic, as it was with Collins and Angela, rather it develops through circumstances of chance that create a familiarity:

> They could not have escaped this even had they wished to, and indeed they did not wish to escape it. They were pawns in the ruthless and complicated games of existence, moved hither and thither on the board by an unseen hand, yet moved side by side, so that they grew to expect each other.
>
> (Hall 82: 287)

The passion is a softer, more protective thing than before and it grows slowly and gently. Stephen wrestles with it, acknowledging her fondness for Mary at the same time as she recalls the past, wary of the trouble it could bring.

Once Mary has to drive with the others, Stephen's concern for her increases and, spending less time together, they each see how vital the other is becoming. 'All roads of thought seemed to lead back to Mary' (Hall, 82: 294). As the war advances, the carnage and pressure increases. Stephen is wounded, and receives a medal. After the presentation ceremony, Mary makes her declaration to Stephen:

> Mary said: 'All my life I've been waiting for something'. 'What was it, my dear?' Stephen asked her gently. And Mary answered: 'I've been waiting for you, and it's seemed such a dreadful long time, Stephen.'. . . 'After the war, no, I won't send you away from me Mary.'
>
> (Hall, 82: 295–6)

This is important and unusual. The theory of lesbianism that imbues the book identifies Mary as a real woman: feminine and capable of heterosexual love and maternity; and as such, quite unlike Stephen. She is just the sort of woman that lesbians are supposed to be attracted to and who sometimes, usually in the absence of a male alternative, will respond to them. It is stressed that such women are merely susceptible, responding to charm and seduction, not that they take initatives to the extent that Mary does, both here and later on that famous night.

Once the war is over and Mary returns to Paris with Stephen,

Stephen Gordon with Other Women

it is unclear on what basis she will be there. They are going to take a holiday together, but are physically restrained although aware of physical attraction: 'So that a touch will stir many secret and perilous emotions ... they sat unnaturally still by the fire, feeling that in their stillness lay safety' (Hall, 82: 300). Mary is more forward, asking for kisses, a request that Stephen complies with but chastely, almost maternally.

By doing so, Stephen is, in her terms, behaving honourably. While Mary may make the decision to commit herself to Stephen, she has to do so when restored from the strains of war. Anything else would be to take advantage of her. During this time, Stephen debates with herself how she should behave with Mary. She asserts a right to lesbian existence much more knowledgeably and with more strength than previously. The relationship she envisages is in many respects positive and here, for the first time in the novel, lesbianism as an opposition and alternative to heterosexuality is clearly stated. It is also one of the few occasions when Stephen acknowledges the idea that she is not alone in her sexuality:

> There was many another exactly like her in this very city, in every city; and they did not all live out crucified lives, denying their bodies, stultifying their brains ... they lived natural lives – lives that to them were perfectly natural.... Men – they were selfish, arrogant, possessive. What could they do for Mary Llewellyn? ... All things they would be the one to the other, should they stand in that limitless relationship; father, mother, friend and lover, all things – the amazing completeness of it:
> (Hall, 82: 302)

Stephen, full of the power to love, is on the verge of going and waking Mary, who has been sent to bed with her cheek quietly kissed. She stops herself, partly with a sense of responsibility towards Mary's state of exhaustion, partly because the vision of sustaining love has to be set against public approbation. Stephen resolves that Mary must be told the risks of loving another woman when and if she makes her declaration.

At this point Stephen's monologue remembers isolation as she practises her declaration to Mary: 'Like Cain, I am marked

Stephen Gordon with Other Women

and blemished' (Hall, 82: 303), a condition she does not envisage Mary shares. In choosing Stephen, Mary will bring the world's wrath down on her: 'Our love may be faithful even unto death and beyond – yet the world will call it unclean' (Hall, 82: 303). Stephen is keenly aware that the world deprives her of the right to protect Mary at exactly the point it is most needed: 'I'm utterly helpless, I can only love you' (Hall, 82: 304).

When, on holiday together, Mary is rebuffed by Stephen's harsh refusals, she acts decisively by saying she will go away. Stephen declares her love for Mary and then utters her warning. Mary counters it. Her desire for Stephen is expressed in the language of rights:

> Mary would want Stephen to take her in her arms, so must rest her cheek against Stephen's shoulder, as though they two had a right to such music, had a right to their share in the love songs of the world.
>
> (Hall, 82: 314)

It is therefore not surprising that her response to Stephen's warnings are equally defiant: 'You can say that – you, who talk about loving! What do I care for the world's opinion? What do I care for anything but you, and you just as you are' (Hall, 82: 316).

The consummation of their love has caused much frustration and conjecture down the years. A recent Cath Tate cartoon made excellent comic mileage out of speculations about what went on in the gap between Chapters 38 and 39. The phrase Radclyffe Hall uses here: '... and that night they were not divided' (Hall, 82: 316), has been seen as evidence of a certain primness, deliberately inexplicit. Its use here is less to do with sexual than emotional concerns. The significance of division, and its absence, is highly charged in a text that has stressed the singularity and isolation of Stephen while at the same time putting marriage, the complementary indivisibility of two people, at the heart of her moral code. As Stephen has struggled to come to terms with her sexual identity, she has been constantly exampled against marriage: her parents, her own, her contemporaries; and against images of harmony, a kind of

Stephen Gordon with Other Women

anthropomorphic marriage, within nature. So, to say that she and Mary were not divided, is to bring their relationship into line with a world from which Stephen has, up to this point, believed herself wholly excluded. The phrase carries with it all the resonance of Stephen's need to belong, to be joined. 'in the grip of Creation ... one at such moments with the fountain of living' (Hall, 82: 317). Also, given the novel's heavy borrowings from biblical imagery, it is impossible to overlook the reference to Saul and Jonathan, a homosexual partnership so strong that 'in their death they were not divided'.

Although there is very little explicit description of sexual activity, the importance of sex is clearly signalled throughout the novel, not just between Mary and Stephen, but also in other sexual partnerships. Looking at Mary, Stephen sees: 'Something quite new in her face, a soft wise expression that Stephen had put there ... the coming of passion' (Hall, 82: 325).

Much later, when their friends Jamie and Barbara die, Mary finds sexual passion reassures some of her own fears about death, a common response to bereavement. She becomes subject to: 'strange amorous moods.... Her kisses would awaken a swift response, and so in these days that were shadowed by death, they clung very desperately to life with the passion they had felt when first they were lovers' (Hall, 82: 410–11).

Finally, during the struggle between Martin and Stephen it is made clear that sex plays a large part in Mary's preference for Stephen: 'The days might be Martin's, but the nights were Stephen's' (Hall, 82: 437). The balance here only shifts when Stephen withholds sex, letting Mary believe that she is having an affair with Valérie. It is at this juncture that Mary, at the height of a quarrel, says that but for Stephen she could have loved Martin Hallam. Stephen acts upon this rather than the misery her rejection is causing, and sets up the chain of events that will result in Mary stumbling heartbroken into Martin's conveniently waiting arms. What Stephen chooses not to hear is the impassioned commitment to her that Mary makes:

> Mary wept and cried out against her: 'I won't let you go – I won't let you. I tell you! It's your fault if I love you the way I do. I can't

Stephen Gordon with Other Women

do without you, you've taught me to need you, and now. . . .' In half-shamed, half-defiant words she must stand there and plead for what Stephen witheld.

(Hall, 82: 439)

Coming so quickly to the end of their relationship is a means, here, simply of illustrating the continuity and importance of the sexual expression of love between them. It is one of the constants in their relationship and, in the history of the novel and its readers, significant in that it establishes the sexual component frankly at a time when writing about lesbianism dwelt on either unspecified corruption or vague companionate relationships.

Their time in Oratava is used to establish their relationship as enriching and positive: 'They were lovers who walked in the vineyard of life. . . . Love had lifted them up as on wings of fire' (Hall, 82: 320). Back in Paris, the lyrical descriptions continue:

> She would wake in the mornings to find Mary beside her, and all through the day she would keep beside Mary, and at night they would lie in each other's arms – God alone knows who shall dare judge of such matters. . . . Life had become a new revelation.
>
> (Hall, 82: 327)

What is most powerful about this relationship is its mutuality. They each come to love freely, without constraints of heterosexual pasts or aspirations. This makes possible a mutual enrichment. Stephen changes Mary, initiating her into physical passion; but Stephen is also changed by Mary, who gives her very ordinary, human, sensual, and material pleasures that have, we realize with something of a shock, been denied Stephen most of her life. She grows: 'Idle and happy and utterly carefree' (Hall, 82: 327).

For the first time, too, Stephen's love has a public expression. Mary will live with her, home includes the person she loves and they spend time out together, able to: 'saunter towards home through streets that were crowded with others who sauntered – men and women, a couple of women together – always twos – the fine nights seemed prolific of couples' (Hall, 82: 328).

Such openness has its limits, though. When Brockett first

Stephen Gordon with Other Women

visits them he is commended, by the narrative voice, for simultaneously understanding and being reticent about the situation between them.

The idyll cannot continue indefinitely, and it is first broken by a summons to Morton from Lady Anna that excludes Mary. Close upon this comes Stephen's need to get back to her writing. Mary's exclusion from Morton is interesting as it provides the first opportunity to see how undermining is the lack of honesty between them, a lack that will ultimately undermine them completely. Within the novel, honesty is the great stumbling block in Mary and Stephen's relationship, a pattern that echoes Stephen's father's stubborn refusal to speak to his daughter and wife.

Stephen does not tell Mary a whole number of things that have been formative in her past. So, Mary does not know about the incident with Angela Crossby, that Stephen was forced to leave Morton, or the nature of Stephen's real relationship with Martin Hallam. Equally, Mary is not shown as asking, so to an extent she colludes in the silences between them. When Stephen first returns to Morton without Mary, her speculation on how impossible it would be to take Mary too centres on the dishonesty it would entail:

> Intolerable quagmire of lies and deceit! The degrading of all that to them was sacred – a very gross degrading of love, and through love a gross degrading of Mary. Mary ... so loyal and yet so gallant, but so pitifully untried in the War of Existence'.
>
> (Hall, 82: 337)

In fact, Mary is quite well aware of the implications of Stephen visiting Morton without her, but she hides this from Stephen. They each keep silent out of a misguided belief that this will protect the other. Again, silence as a form of protection picks up the thread of her father's misguided behaviour early in the novel. It becomes a defining characteristic of Stephen: something that formed her and that she perpetuates, despite the damage it does. This is clearly recognized by and commented upon by the narrative.

As Stephen's life settles back into its routines, with some

Stephen Gordon with Other Women

accommodation to Mary's presence, Mary, who has no activity or work, becomes increasingly isolated. It is not just this material inequality between them that undermines their relationship, but their inability to acknowledge it.

> If only Stephen had confided in her.... But no, she shrank from reminding the girl of the gloom that surrounded their small patch of sunshine.... And thus, blinded by love and her desire to protect the woman she loved, she erred towards Mary.
>
> (Hall, 82: 346)

Eventually, and largely in response to Mary's isolation, they become part of the lesbian life in Paris, forming a particular friendship with Barbara and Jamie, whose relationship seems at times a version of Stephen and Mary's without the money. Jamie, like Stephen, took to boyish ways as a child and was indulged and protected by a loving father. She is also highly gifted, with musical talents. After her father's death hostility drives her away from a home that she continues to mourn the loss of. When Barbara dies of tuberculosis, Jamie kills herself because: 'She dared not go home to Beadles for fear of shaming the woman she loved' (Hall, 82: 409). Barbara and Mary develop a rather fussy feminine friendship based on sharing the attempt to care for and succour their talented, self-neglecting partners. Playing at wives to their men.

Stephen and Mary's support and community with others is not highly valued, it is defensive rather than a positive move towards this new life style. They each experience the life quite separately and do not communicate that to each other. In this way, something that could ground and strengthen their relationship ultimately drives a wedge into it:

> They were launched upon the stream that flows silent and deep through all great cities, gliding on between precipitous borders, away and away into no-man's-land – the most desolate country in all creation. Yet when they got home they felt no misgivings.
>
> (Hall, 82: 360)

There is a curious double presentation of the thing as deeply depressing and gloom-laden, yet also positive, a source of

Stephen Gordon with Other Women

pleasure. Also, obliquely, and in some cases directly, the message of lesbianism's all-pervasiveness is being relayed. The assumption that this 'stream' exists in all great cities.

A crisis befalls them from which Stephen is unable to protect Mary. A holiday friendship is abruptly terminated once the true nature of their relationship with each other is known. Having guessed the content of Lady Massey's letter, Mary snatches it from Stephen's hand, reads for herself their rejection. Their distress at this does not bring them closer together. Stephen, who makes the dangerous assumption that Mary's happiness is her responsibility, is unable to comfort or console her. Although the incident sparks both the statement and expression of their love for each other, it is not presented positively: 'She seemed to be striving to obliterate not only herself, but the whole hostile world through some strange and agonised merging with Mary' (Hall, 82: 376). Sexual passion becomes almost a weapon against each other and a scourge to themselves. Sex becomes the site of the world's pressures upon them.

It is social rejection that turns them to the company of their lesbian friends,

> Mary seemed frantically eager to proclaim her allegiances to Pat's miserable army. Deprived of the social intercourse which to her would have been both natural and welcome, she now strove to stand up to a hostile world by proving that she could get on without it.
>
> (Hall, 82: 384)

This is very slanted. By referring to it as 'Pat's army', we are focused onto the least positive of all the women – Pat who: 'Collected her moths and her beetles, and when fate was propitious an occasional woman. But fate was so seldom propitious to Pat (Hall, 82: 359).

Mary starts to drink, something in the text that indicates moral decline. She coarsens and hardens under the pressure: 'Pretended to a callousness that, in truth, she was very far from feeling. . . . "Beggars can't be choosers in this world, Stephen!" ' (Hall, 82: 396). Mary copes with the pressure in a way that will,

Stephen Gordon with Other Women

ultimately, lower her self-esteem; she does not hold herself apart from the bars and the circle's drinking and forced gaiety as does Stephen. For Stephen, their social life forges her sense of destiny. She suffers, but it is a redemptive suffering, highly moral and ultimately transcendent. They do not speak to each other about this. Instead Stephen talks with Valérie, working out with her a theory of lesbian life that could have been more constructively shared with Mary.

After the deaths of Barbara and Jamie, Stephen deliberately switches her confidences from Mary to Valérie:

> Like most inverts she found a passing relief in discussing the intolerable situation; in dissecting it ruthlessly, bit by bit, even though she arrived at no solution, but since Jamie's death it did not seem wise to dwell too much on this subject with Mary.
>
> (Hall, 82: 411)

The relationship between Mary and Stephen appears stretched and stressed, mutually evasive and alienated. It is thus weakened when Martin Hallam arrives to bring a different relief to each of them. For Stephen, Martin provides something she has been missing for a long time, a friendship that was: 'Just accepting her now for the thing that she was, without question, and accepting most of her friends with a courtesy as innocent of patronage as of any suspicion of morbid interest' (Hall, 82: 424). For Mary, his presence enables them to participate in normal life: social visits to the Comtesse de Mirac; fashionable cafes; dancing: 'Reassured by the presence of Martin Hallam, re-established in pride and self-respect she was able to contemplate the world without her erstwhile sense of isolation' (Hall, 82: 428).

At first, Martin is presented as harmonizing their relationship, but gradually his presence shifts the balance. He is not simply a person, a friend, but an embodiment of heterosexuality and as such threatens and undermines what Stephen and Mary have. Initially, Martin experiences this as conflict spread equally between his responsibility towards both women: 'He could not bring about Stephen's destruction – and yet, if he spared her, he might destroy Mary' (Hall, 82: 432), but it is only

Stephen Gordon with Other Women

a matter of time before he shifts squarely towards Mary, whose interests he identifies with his own.

The consequences of this for Mary and Stephen are explored through the effect upon their sexual relationship. This is a further instance of how powerful is the sexual theme in the novel, an indication of the extent to which it is at the centre of their connection to each other. However, even within this powerful intimacy, they are still silenced, unable to communicate with each other:

> Stephen's masterful arms would enfold the warm softness of Mary's body, the while she would be shaken as though with great cold. Lying there she would shiver with terror and love, and this torment of hers would envelop Mary so that sometimes she wept for the pain of it all, yet neither would give a name to that torment.
>
> (Hall, 82: 432)

These silences build into their relationship, eroding it. The only moment at which what is happening between them is confronted is when Stephen lies to Mary about Valérie Seymour; a lie that she perpetrates by omission, allowing Mary to believe something that is untrue: ' "With Valérie Seymour. I thought you'd know somehow.... It's better to be frank ... we both hate lies." "... and I've tried so hard not to believe it! Tell me you're lying to me now"' (Hall, 82: 444). This is the final exchange between them, Stephen's silence forces Mary out of the house, out of the relationship. Outside, carefully primed by Stephen, Martin waits. So, a relationship that has consistently failed to address honesty ends in a mixture of manipulated dishonesty. The significance is twofold. First, a salutory lesson in the importance of truthfulness and trust between women, a highlighting of how, given the pressure outside lesbian relationships to silence and undermine, there is an even greater premium upon honesty within them. Second, the passage of Mary from Stephen, and homosexuality, to Martin and heterosexuality is shown as anything but natural and inevitable. On the contrary, Mary has to be prised away from Stephen.

79

Stephen Gordon with Other Women

But, as has been noted elsewhere, the text of *The Well of Loneliness* is a complex and contradictory one. The unhappy ending is undermined by the manipulation needed to effect it and by the clear, oppositional voice of Valérie Seymour, as well as all the other points in the novel where an alternative view is being put. That the novel is pulled towards the tragic and melodramatic is linked with Stephen's character.

Whereas the early sections of the novel hinted at doom to come for Stephen on account of her lesbianism, which remained hidden from her until well into it, now the presentiment of disaster is linked to her: 'Inherent respect of the normal ... handed down by the silent and watchful founders of Morton' (Hall, 82: 438). The restatement of how firmly heterosexuality is rooted in Stephen's moral code and vision of peace and security accompanies her realization that she can never fulfill it. She believes she cannot love as she should, as her parents did, and that part of her character that associates love with service and suffering convinces her that the fullest expression of her love for Mary is to make her: 'The gift of Martin' (Hall, 82: 439). How Mary may feel about this is not an issue. There is no history, and therefore no expectation of such discussions and honesty between them.

Valerie, who is implicated in Stephen's course of action, is consulted and has the task of opposing Stephen. Although Stephen does not take Valerie's advice, it is important that the book contains her reasoned argument: 'Aren't you being absurdly self-sacrificing? You can give the girl a very great deal.... Protection! Protection! I'm sick of the word. Let her do without it; aren't you enough for her?' (Hall, 82: 443).

The melodrama is played out, with Stephen represented as being in some kind of trance. This both increases the tension of the scheme and strengthens the impact of Stephen's divine role as the voice that will plead: 'Acknowledge us, oh God, before the whole world. Give us also the right to our existence!' (Hall, 82: 447). At the same time, the broken delirium of Mary's actual departure from the house in a sense absolves Stephen from responsibility for it: 'A mist closing down ... what was the figure doing in the mist ... Going? Going? But where could

Stephen Gordon with Other Women

it go? Somewhere out of the mist, somewhere into the light' (Hall, 82: 445).

It is Stephen's sense of honour that dictates this course of action, a sense of honour passed to her from her father, a moral code that, fifty years later, Adrienne Rich was to expose as useless for women in *Some notes on honour and lying*, which reads at times like a gloss upon Stephen's actions and motives:

> The old, male idea of honour. A man's 'word' sufficed – to other men – without guarantee.... Male honour also having something to do with killing ... something needing to be avenged.... Patriarchal lying has manipulated women both through falsehood and through silence. Facts we needed have been witheld from us ... lying is done with words, and also with silences.
>
> (Rich, 79: 1)

The significance of silence, the inability of Mary and Stephen to speak the truth of their relationship and fight for it, is returned to at the novel's climax. When Stephen returns to the house after her night away, she has to struggle through silence, a silence made palpable: 'Articulate silence that leapt out shouting from every corner – a jibing, grimacing, vindictive silence. She brushed it aside with a sweep of her hand' (Hall, 82: 444).

The Well of Loneliness, through publication, broke through a silence about lesbian lives; Stephen herself is articulate about the nature of the condition, but it is left to the book's readers, and to future generations to articulate the possibility of lesbian lives in partnership. The idea that lesbians can live happily, or at all, together is one that appears very infrequently in the novel.

WOMEN IN THE WORLD

We follow the progress of Stephen in relation to other women, although none of these relationships endure. We are given insights particularly into the powerful long-term relationship between Barbara and Jamie, but this ends with them each dying

Stephen Gordon with Other Women

young. Apart from that, we encounter lesbians either as being single, or as being engaged in brief, shallow affairs. Because Stephen is so central to the narrative of *The Well of Loneliness* and therefore in defining what it is to be a lesbian, it is important to stress how the presence of other strands in the text contribute to opening out the discourse around what it is to be a lesbian.

Stephen's orientation is always towards the heterosexual world, against which she pitches her arguments and plea for tolerance and acceptance. Within the homosexual world, she is reluctant to see connections and community and appears at times almost wilful in her refusal to recognize the existence of other lesbians. Where such recognition is unavoidable, as with Valérie Seymour, Stephen's initial responses are hostile and suspicious, although this does change. The whole progress of that friendship is significant: Valérie is the only woman with whom the adult Stephen has anything approximating to an equal relationship. Behind it lie years of distance from women to whom Stephen can relate to only in the unequal terms of the beloved and lover, servant and served; or as a detached observer.

The war, which was of tremendous significance in various struggles for women's emancipation, is decisive in *The Well of Loneliness*. Things after it are never the same, and it is after the war, with Mary, that Stephen comes fully into lesbian identity. At its outset, Stephen is angry because of her exclusion from the war: 'She was nothing but a freak abandoned on a kind of no-man's-land at this moment of splendid national endeavour' (Hall, 82: 271). The shrewd Puddle, however, is of a different opinion; one that turns out to be in fact correct, that: 'This war may give your sort of woman her chance' (Hall, 82: 271). We gain a sense of how numerous, and ordinary, lesbian life is and can be as Stephen observes:

> Unmistakable figures ... Miss Smith who had been breeding dogs in the country; or Miss Oliphant who had been breeding nothing since birth but a litter of hefty complexes; or Miss Tring who had lived with a very dear friend in the humbler purlieus of Chelsea.
>
> (Hall, 82: 274)

Stephen Gordon with Other Women

All the same, there is no sense of solidarity and everything is overshadowed by the war, an act of such unnatural social life that it sanctions or tolerates abnormality of all kinds, not on their own terms, but as they can be utilized:

> As though gaining courage from the terror that is war, many a one who was even as Stephen had crept out of her hole and come into the daylight.... And England had taken her, asking no questions – she was strong and efficient, she could fill a man's place.
>
> (Hall, 82: 274)

It is, however, not entirely one-sided, the text goes on to speak of: 'A battalion was formed in those terrible years that would never again be completely disbanded ... never again would such women submit to being driven back to their holes and corners. They had found themselves' (Hall, 82: 275). Found themselves, but not each other. Such women, too, are seen at a distance, they do not appear as part of the unit that Stephen eventually joins.

WOMEN AS FRIENDS

It is as an observer that Stephen relates to lesbian Paris. Her second visit to Valérie Seymour's salon, this time with Mary, provides the opportunity to scan and categorize the assembled company. Stephen changes her opinion of Valérie Seymour. Whereas previously she was angered at being perceived simply in terms of her sexual identity, it is precisely that that she now enjoys:

> Stephen could not get rid of the feeling that everyone knew about her and Mary, or that if they did not actually know, they guessed, and were eager to show themselves friendly. She thought: 'Well, why not? I'm sick of lying.'
>
> (Hall, 82: 353)

The desire to see everyone as types indicates how powerful were the biological theories of sexuality to which Stephen subscribes.

Stephen Gordon with Other Women

At the same time, these types overlap, engender confusion:

> The grades were so numerous and so fine that they often defied the most careful observation. The timbre of a voice, the build of an ankle, the texture of a hand, a movement, a gesture – since few were so pronounced as Stephen Gordon.
>
> (Hall 82: 356)

Biology is not a reliable index of sexuality. At the centre of this gathering is Valérie: 'Placid and self-assured [she] created an atmosphere of courage, everyone felt very normal and brave when they gathered together' (Hall, 82: 356). A far cry from the evil associations of decadence and immorality that Stephen first associated with her. In the context of this circle, Valérie occupies its moral centre, especially in her abhorrence of drink and drugs. A discourse on love, presented as Stephen's reflections, but in fact knowing far more about everyone than she possibly could at this stage, emphasizes the misery of lesbian life. Stephen's identification with it all is ambiguous: 'To her own kind she turned and was made very welcome, for no bond is more binding than that of affliction. But her vision stretched beyond to the day when happier folk would also accept her' (Hall, 82: 360).

Stephen and Mary hold themselves apart from lesbian life until Lady Massey's rejection of their friendship, which evokes Stephen's original banishment from Morton. Then, as if with nothing to lose, they throw themselves headlong into Parisian lesbian nightlife and the novel takes us with them on a visit to bars and clubs in the company of a new generation of lesbians, such as Dickie, the aviator, who are: 'More reckless, more aggressive and self-assured . . . refusing point-blank to believe in the existence of a miserable army. They said: " We are as we are; what about it? We don't give a damn, in fact we're delighted." ' (Hall, 82: 387). The standards of this new lesbian existence are still perceived as being male. Dickie is described as looking like a schoolboy, aiming to: 'Outdo men in their sinning' (Hall, 82: 387). The authorial tone here is indulgent: they think they've escaped but they haven't. They'll suffer, just let them grow up a bit.

Stephen Gordon with Other Women

Stephen envies Valérie's detachment from her surroundings during this journey around the bars and their attendant depravity. It is this that draws Stephen to her, the direct opposite of Stephen's reforming zeal. They discuss the nature of lesbianism. Valérie's approach is sanguine, pragmatic, and as such provides a foil to Stephen. Valerie is useful to Stephen, giving her what no-one else ever has, which is a kind of sanctuary. The friendship that develops between them is one that hitherto Stephen only looked for from men, a situation that involves denying her lesbianism: 'You'll never know the relief it is to have someone to talk to' (Hall, 82: 414).

Valérie's amused interest in Stephen is valuable in indicating how far to take Stephen as the lesbian norm. This serves as a useful check against the temptation to see Stephen as the archetypal lesbian, her way of living that out as the only one. Valérie is skilled in human psychology and experienced in the many versions of lesbian existence. It is she who, in her appraisal of Stephen, confirms her distance from the mainstream of lesbianism, identifies the particular conflict she experiences: 'You're rather a terrible combination; you've the nerves of the abnormal with all that they stand for ... and then ... you've all the respectable country instincts of the man who cultivates children and acres' (Hall, 82: 414).

Such oppositions intrigue Valerie. She is indulgent of them, interested in what Stephen makes of them, and identifies her oddness less as a feature of her sexual identity than of her class position. It is the degree of trust and understanding between the two women that is explored here, which adds the necessary authority to Valérie's protestation that Stephen's action in forcing Mary to leave is foolish.

The Well of Loneliness sometimes seems to exist only as an exercise in the impossibility of relationships between women, and of being a woman and a lesbian. The very terms seem to be in opposition. Within those difficulties, Valerie Seymour illustrates the ideal of detached self-sufficiency, which is of limited value in establishing a positive identity for lesbians.

It is untrue to assert that lesbianism is defined only by physical, sexual involvements with other women. However, it

Stephen Gordon with Other Women

is also important, especially in the context of *The Well of Loneliness*, to be aware that isolation is usually imposed upon lesbians, their singular states often not chosen. Valerie may choose to prioratize independence; others, including Puddle, have it thrust upon them.

Puddle is one of the most consistent voices for tolerance heard in the book, yet her dialogue is almost exclusively with the reader. The fact of her own lesbianism, which is clearly located in the past, is never properly acknowledged by Stephen.

After Martin Hallam's departure, it is Puddle who sustains Stephen, trying to toughen her up. She is angry with Anna, who does not comfort Stephen, but even more so with Sir Philip: 'Who knew the whole truth, or so she suspected, and who yet kept that truth back' (Hall, 82: 111). The strength of her emotion comes in part from having undergone similar experiences: 'Puddle would flush with reminiscent anger as her mind slipped back and back over the years to old sorrows, old miseries, long decently buried but now disinterred by this pitiful Stephen' (Hall, 82: 111).

After Sir Philip's death, when Stephen decides not to follow through her plans to go to Oxford, she goes against Puddle's advice. Puddle rails against the conspiracy of silence surrounding Stephen, but also contributes to it: 'She dared not explain the girl to herself' (Hall, 82: 121).

Although Stephen is denied Puddle's straightforward, reasonable opinions about lesbianism throughout the novel, they are available to the reader and form a vein of strong and positive commentary upon lesbianism: 'Outrageous, Puddle would feel it to be, that wilfully selfish tyranny of silence evolved by a crafty old ostrich of a world for its own well-being and comfort' (Hall, 82: 121).

At the height of her suffering over Angela, Stephen is unable to confide in Puddle: 'Who could have given much wise advice' (Hall, 82: 153), and Puddle:

Loathed and despised the conspiracy of silence that forbade her to speak frankly. The conspiracy of silence that had sent the girl forth unprotected, right into the arms of this woman. A vain

Stephen Gordon with Other Women

shallow woman in search of excitement.

(Hall, 82: 153)

Puddle struggles with the need to keep silent and her increasingly strong desire to break that silence. In doing so she is motivated partly by her sense of loyalty and love for Stephen and partly by the memories of her own suffering as a young woman: 'Her youth would come back and stare into her eyes reproachfully' (Hall, 82: 155).

What ultimately forced her to keep her counsel is knowing that by speaking out she runs the risk of being sent away by Lady Anna, her employer. Because of the social inequality in their relationship, Puddle is unable to make available to Stephen some of the most important knowledge she has, far greater than any she has acquired from Oxford. Again, though, her imagined speech to Stephen is presented in full and serves as a useful counter to the tragic excesses of Stephen's actual relationship with Angela:

> You're neither unnatural, nor abominable, nor mad; you're as much a part of what people call nature as anyone else ... meanwhile don't shrink from yourself, but just face yourself calmly and bravely. Have courage; ... show the world that people like you and they can be quite as selfless and fine as the rest of mankind.

(Hall, 82: 153)

Although Puddle thinks like this, her actual life represents the complete denial of her lesbianism, so her positive contributions are always undermined by her own example and her extreme uncomfortableness whenever Stephen advances towards the company of other lesbians: 'Like to like. No, no, an intolerable thought ... and yet, after all what else? What remained? Loneliness or worse still, far worse because it so deeply degraded the spirit, a life of perpetual subterfuge' (Hall, 82: 244). The conflict she articulates here, must link to the painful awareness that what has been denied her could become a reality for another, younger generation.

Whatever Puddle's ambivalences are, she never expresses them to Stephen, who she consistently supports in times of

87

Stephen Gordon with Other Women

crisis. When Lady Anna forces Stephen to leave Morton, it is Puddle who transforms that into a moment of heroics. Stephen is too overcome to fully take in Puddle's statement that: 'all that you're suffering at this moment I've suffered. It was when I was very young like you – but I still remember' (Hall, 82: 207). Indeed, the text emphasizes that: 'She had not understood Puddle's meaning' (Hall, 82: 208). What is made clear, is the commitment to work, the sense of purpose that rescues Stephen's departure from Morton from absolute negativity. It is Puddle who first articulates Stephen's destiny, who does, in fact, come to explain her to herself: 'For the sake of all the others who are like you, but less strong and less gifted perhaps, many of them, it's up to you to have the courage to make good' (Hall, 82: 208).

Puddle does then dedicate her life to the care and support of Stephen, though her sustaining role refers only to her writing; she does not offer counsel on how to live as a lesbian. When Stephen experiences despair because of her sexuality:

> There's a great chunk of life that I've never known, and I want to know it. I ought to know it if I'm to become a really fine writer ... why should I live in this great isolation of spirit and body ... why have I been afflicted with a body that must never be indulged.
>
> (Hall, 82: 217)

Puddle cannot answer her: 'Having no comfort, that is, that she dared to offer' (Hall, 82: 217).

It is interesting to speculate here what exactly it is that Puddle does not dare to offer. Is it perhaps her theory about making good for the sake of others, which under the circumstances seems a little besides the point. Or perhaps Puddle is unwilling to encourage Stephen to look for lesbian love, unable to speak of it, because of her strong feelings for Stephen. Whatever her reasons, nothing is said and Stephen's crisis that she: 'Will never be a great writer because of my maimed and insufferable body' (Hall, 82: 217) is not resolved until they decide to move to Paris.

Paris is a trial to Puddle. She is too old for it and is anxious

Stephen Gordon with Other Women

about Stephen's motives for wishing to be there. When Stephen settles to a life in Paris as isolated as that in London: 'Puddle could not make up her mind whether she felt relieved or regretful' (Hall, 82: 258).

During the war they both return to London and when Stephen goes abroad, Puddle, much against her will, returns to Morton. After the war, without being told directly, Puddle grasps the nature of the relationship with Mary and decides to stay on at Morton. Again, her sense of what is happening is conflicting. Her reason for staying is knowing: 'Her presence in Paris would only embarrass while unable to hinder. Nothing could stay fate if the hour had struck; and yet, from the very bottom of her soul, she was fearing that hour for Stephen' (Hall, 82: 306).

Yet at the same time, she is capable of transcending the limits imposed by her own experience, wanting Stephen to transcend them too:

> And who shall presume to accuse or condemn? – she actually found it in her to pray that Stephen might be granted some measure of fulfilment, some palliative for the wound of existence: 'Not like me – don't let her grow old as I've done.'
>
> (Hall, 82: 306)

This is the last contribution Puddle makes to the novel. Her role has been to sustain Stephen but also to offer, contrapunctally, another version of lesbianism that although low-key in its expectations, has a certain optimism and satisfaction to it. It is lesbianism transposed from the selfish and self-indulgent to selfless service for others. For many lesbians this selflessness is part of their experience, though frequently linked, as is Puddle's, to the obligation upon them, as single women, to earn a living and make their way in the world.

Stephen's relationships with women are complex and varied. They are central to her life but she appears to accord them less status than she does her relationship with men. The distaste about women and femininity is a major factor in rendering this book, and the character of Stephen Gordon, difficult for a contemporary lesbian readership.

Chapter Four

HOW DOES THE READER GET ON WITH STEPHEN GORDON?

W HAT READERS make of Stephen Gordon has depended upon their access to the novel, something which has not always been assured. *The Well of Loneliness* was though sufficiently capable of influencing its readers to warrant being banned for obscenity in 1928, shortly after publication. This history of publication is an important dimension and I will consider it in some detail.

The question of readers and the novel, particularly in terms of the character of Stephen Gordon, has to address the lesbian reader as distinct from the heterosexual reader. *The Well of Loneliness* was clearly written for heterosexuals and it is interesting to consider how far Radclyffe Hall achieved her stated aim of generating sympathy and understanding for lesbians.

Despite Radclyffe Hall's orientation towards its heterosexual readership, the book is most widely read by lesbians and it is this that most interests me. I have drawn upon the results of a survey I carried out into readership and have also consulted a similar survey organized by the New York Lesbian Herstory Archive in 1986. Through this it is possible to begin constructing a picture of how *The Well of Loneliness* has been used and valued within lesbian lives.

In her account of their life together, Una, Lady Troubridge, states that Radclyffe Hall had wanted to tackle the theme of lesbianism in her writing for some time. She felt responsible towards Una when she did start work, but believed her

How does the Reader get on with Stephen Gordon?

reputation was such that the book would neither damage her standing nor remain obscure. It was published in 1928, some 22 years after the start of Radclyffe Hall's writing career and was promoted in a way carefully designed to minimize negative reactions. Once Radclyffe Hall overcame her hesitation about writing the book, she then encountered difficulty in finding a publisher.

Both Cassells and Heinemann, who had published her previously, refused it on the grounds that it could damage them. Secker turned it down on the grounds that it would prove uncommercial, although at the time they were in the process of bringing out Compton McKenzie's *Extraordinary Women*, a satire on continental lesbian society.

Cape finally agreed to take the novel but on terms quite different from usual. It was to be published in a limited edition of 1,250 copies which would sell for 25 shillings, approximately three times the average price of a novel. This, and the decision to publish the book in a plain jacket and send it for review only to the serious dailies and periodicals, suggests an attempt to avoid sensationalism and an eschewing of mass markets. In the event, the book's initial print run was for 1,500 copies at 15 shillings and a second edition was in preparation when action was taken against the book.

American publishers were no less cautious. Doubleday and Harper turned the book down, making it quite clear that they objected to the subject matter and Knopf, who accepted, inserted a clause into the original contract that left the author liable for any legal actions against the book. This clause was eventually deleted. It is clear, from references in Una's account and other biographical sources, that Radclyffe Hall had a clear sense of moral purpose in writing *The Well of Loneliness*. Michael Baker, in *Our Three Selves* quotes from a letter Radclyffe wrote Una's brother-in-law, editor of the *Observer*: 'Many writers have been nibbling at it just lately in fiction – but this I have felt to be wrong and only calculated to awaken in certain minds an unwholesome and salacious curiosity' (Baker, 1985: 209).

Publication day was 27 July 1928 and the first crop of

How does the Reader get on with Stephen Gordon?

reviews, mostly by men in publications such as the *Nation*, the *Tatler*, *Time and Tide*, etc. appear to have treated the novel respectfully and seriously. It was generally well received by such writers as Leonard Woolf, L. P. Hartley, and Vera Brittain, who nevertheless agreed that the polemic rather weakened the novel's case. The book sold well, was into its second printing by the second week of August, and Una writes of their pleasure in seeing it displayed in the window of W. H. Smith. Whatever misgivings there were about the novel, they seem to have centred on its literary qualities, with most people finding it inferior to Radclyffe Hall's other publications. Less than a month later, the *Sunday Express* launched a carefully orchestrated attack under the headline: 'A Book That Must Be Suppressed'.

The comments on this occurrence by the novelist E. F. Benson, himself part of the homosexual literary clique, are interesting. Writing in *As We Are*, a memoir first published in 1930, he makes it clear that the theme of homosexuality had already emerged in literature. His observations strengthen the argument that opposition to Radclyffe Hall came from a sense of moral outrage that she would neither offer homosexuality up for heterosexual mockery and entertainment, as Compton Mackenzie did, nor condemn it. He writes:

> Book after book appeared in which it was introduced without disguise or reprehension, ... the topic appeared, no longer *pour rire*, but as the basis of a serious study, in Miss Radclyffe Hall's *The Well of Loneliness.* ... It was in its 2nd edition when a certain journalist (the time of the year being the 'silly season' of early August) started a crusading campaign against it ... he assured his readers that he would prefer to put a phial of prussic acid into a girl's hands than let her read it.... It is one of the saddest books in the world, painting as it does in the most convincing colours the misery and loneliness. ... The book is its own antidote against the poison it was supposed to contain: it is impossible to imagine a stronger deterrent.
>
> (Benson, 1985: 263–5)

The initial impact was to increase interest and sales; one London library reported receiving 600 enquiries about the book

How does the Reader get on with Stephen Gordon?

on Monday 20 August. It is arguable that had Cape handled the situation better, then the subsequent trial and ban would never have happened. Cape responded to the debate in the press, where the *Daily Express* was pitted against the *Daily Herald*, by offering to submit the book for the Home Secretary's approval. This was a completely voluntary act and mimicked the legislation that did affect playwrights at the time whose work had to be licensed by the Lord Chamberlain, a restriction that remained in force until the late 1960s. Sir William Joyson-Hix, termed 'The Policeman of the Lord' in Beresford Egan's scurrilous satire on the trial, was a fundamentalist Christian who had already expressed concern over the proliferation of immoral literature. Needless to say, he did not approve of *The Well of Loneliness* and Cape, again voluntarily and under no threat from any kind of prosecution, withdrew copies of the book and cancelled its third reprinting. Neither Radclyffe Hall nor her literary agent were consulted about these moves.

Knopf immediately halted publication in America. They did eventually go ahead and an action was brought against the book in New York, when it was in its sixth edition. The case against it was not found. Meanwhile, Cape had arranged to have the book printed in Paris and imported back into Britain for sale. Copies were seized by customs in October, but as the book was not the subject of any legal proceedings and had been voluntarily withdrawn, it was eventually released. Shortly afterwards, both Cape and the bookshop that had imported the stock were raided and charges were laid under the 1857 *Obscene Publications Act.*

Attempts to organize a defence were hampered by rumours that Cape had deliberately allowed the action to be brought as part of a publicity stunt. More difficult was the confusion as to who exactly was on trial for what: the book, the publishers, or the author and many literary figures who should have engaged with the question of censorship did not do so. Some writers felt compromised by having to defend a book that they found to be lacking in literary worth, though a significant number, including Virginia Woolf, saw the necessity of putting those scruples to one side. In the event, witnesses for the defence were

How does the Reader get on with Stephen Gordon?

not called. An area of support rarely acknowledged is one that the *Daily Herald* mobilized, particularly from the National Union of Railwaymen and the South Wales Miners' Federation. It is important to realize that such coalitions predate our contemporary politics.

Radclyffe Hall received enormous public support, mostly in the form of letters, of which she is rumoured to have received 10,000 around the time of the publication and trial of *The Well of Loneliness*. On 1 September 1928 alone she received 400 letters. Were they available, those letters would make an enormous contribution to our knowledge of attitudes towards lesbianism and to how women experienced and identified with the plight of both Stephen Gordon and Radclyffe Hall. The experience confirmed Radclyffe Hall's own sense of the rightness of what she had done. Although she was never allowed to put her defence in court, it is a powerful document:

> I do not regret having written the book. All that has happened has only served to show me how badly my book was needed. I am proud to have written *The Well of Loneliness*, and I would not alter so much as a comma.
>
> (quoted in Baker, 1985: 238)

While the trial brought the novel to the attention of many more people than might otherwise have taken notice of it, actual access to the book was still difficult. After 1928 it was possible to acquire copies in English from either America or Paris but this hardly constituted wide availability. The existing 3,000 copies in circulation would have had a limited readership and it wasn't until the 1960s that a paperback edition appeared. The novel was reprinted twice by the Falcon Press in 1949, then in 1950, and again three times in 1952. This ensured a wider circulation and secured *The Well of Loneliness* in its status as an underground classic. By the late 1950s it appears as part of the uniform reprint edition of Radclyffe Hall's work that Hammond & Hammond brought out and various editions followed throughout the 1960s and 70s until in 1982 Virago, the feminist publisher who have done most to reclaim and re-evaluate traditions of women's writing, brought out an edition with

How does the Reader get on with Stephen Gordon?

a fine contextualizing introduction by Alison Hennegan that finally delivered *The Well of Loneliness* to a contemporary lesbian-feminist readership.

Many critics see Radclyffe Hall as a one-book author: a writer too closely identified with *The Well of Loneliness*. They view it as unfortunate that she is associated with lesbianism, finding it detracts from and distorts the real writing concerns she has; lesbian readers are often disappointed that in her other writing the impact of her own lesbian existence is muted and subdued.

The Well of Loneliness is not an aberration in Radclyffe Hall's writing career. Radclyffe Hall came late to novels: her earliest writing and publishing was of poetry, initially through vanity presses. In 1906 she published 'Twixt Earth and Stars', in 1908 'A Sheaf of Verses', in 1910 'Poems of Past and Present', in 1913 'Songs of Three Counties', and in 1915 'The Forgotten Island'. In the main they are lyrical and pastoral verses of no great significance, though extremely popular at the time and were often, as was 'The Blind Ploughman', set to music. Reviews of her poetry read very oddly alongside the later reputation:

> Some composers of music have found certain of Miss Hall's verses delightfully singable, so that the drawing-room is doubtless duly thankful to her and them. Her poems are fresh in sentiment, simple and tender in expression, and quite free from hot-house luxuriances.
>
> (*Yorkshire Post*, 8 October 1913)

> They abound in a tender twilight atmosphere, and in the fresh clear romance of the countryside.... Miss Radclyffe-Hall has the true lyric touch, and, what is more, her simple emotion speaks straight from heart to heart.
>
> (The *Daily Telegraph*, 14 March 1913)

A good many of her poems, particularly in 'A Sheaf of Verses', are quite clearly about relationships with women. That she could be so popular whilst writing poems such as an 'Ode to Sappho' and To _____

How does the Reader get on with Stephen Gordon?

> Our little love is newly born
> And shall I say goodbye?
> For if I go, perchance ere dawn
> Our little love will die!
>
> I'd better stay and help it grow,
> Since it is yours and mine,
> Until this little love we know
> Becomes a love divine.

is a testament to the invisibility of lesbians and the unthinkable nature of lesbianism. Her poetry was also undoubtedly popular with women who knew exactly what she was writing about, one of the more celebrated of whom was the singer Mabel Batten, who put many of the poems to music. Known as Ladye, she was her first serious lover, the third self to whom her writing was always dedicated. After 1924, when Radclyffe Hall began writing prose fiction, no more poetry was published and possibly none was written.

The first novel that Radclyffe Hall wrote was *The Unlit Lamp*. Its theme is frustrated ambition and there is a clear, if inexplicit, lesbian theme. According to Lovat Dickson, who is the most unreliable of her biographers, it was refused by ten publishers before Cassells took it in 1924. That year also saw *The Forge* published, followed in 1925 by *A Saturday Life*, a remarkable Hall novel in that it sets out to be and succeeds in being very funny. In 1926 *Adam's Breed*, a novel about an Italian waiter, was published and this won both the Prix Femina and the James Tait Black Prize in 1927. It was on the back of these achievements that Radclyffe Hall risked writing *The Well of Loneliness*.

The outcry that *The Well of Loneliness* provoked took its toll on her. Much of her distress stemmed from an anxiety that the book could be construed as blasphemous. She took particular exception to Beresford Egan's Satire *The Sink of Solitude*, which included some rather unpleasant drawings of her semi-naked and crucified. Her sense of insult had been less for herself than for the Lord. *The Master of the House*, which came out in 1932, was a rewriting and updating of the story of Christ and whilst working on it Radclyffe Hall suffered a skin disease,

How does the Reader get on with Stephen Gordon?

which she and Una interpreted as a sign from God: the stigmata.

In 1934 a collection of short stories entitled *Miss Ogilvy Finds Herself* appeared. The title story to some extent tried out the character of Stephen Gordon. It was written in July 1926 and is described in the foreword thus:

> Although Miss Ogilvy is a very different person from Stephen Gordon, yet those who have read *The Well of Loneliness* will find in the earlier part of this story the nucleus of those sections of my novel which deal with Stephen Gordon's childhood and girlhood, and with the noble and selfless work done by hundreds of sexually inverted women during the Great War.
>
> (Hall, 1934: Foreword)

In 1936 the final novel, *The Sixth Beatitude*, was published. After Radclyffe Hall's death in 1943, Una carried out her wishes and destroyed the manuscript she was working on at the time. Some speculation exists as to whether or not this work had a lesbian theme. Una appears quite definite about it: '*The Well of Loneliness* contained all that she had to say on that subject; that she had never for a moment contemplated a sequel or any return to that aspect of nature' (Troubridge, 1961: 171).

With the exception of her poetry, which has not attracted the same attention, all of her novels have been republished at least once. Virago have republished *A Saturday Life, The Unlit Lamp*, and *Adam's Breed*, in addition to *The Well of Loneliness*. 'A Sheaf of Verses', some of the best and most explicitly lesbian of Radclyffe Hall's poetry was republished in a private limited edition in 1985.

The Well of Loneliness frequently appears in new editions, and its presentation provides interesting material. What image of lesbianism does the book seek to promote and to what extent is the book being seen as a serious or pornographic treatment? I have not had access to many different editions of *The Well of Loneliness* but those I have seen demonstrate some considerable range.

It was first published in 1928 with a plain black cover and lettered title and author. This minimalist style was fairly common at the time. The other versions I have seen are a 1960s

How does the Reader get on with Stephen Gordon?

paperback, presenting a version of 'The English Rose' *circa* 1950. The two women are blonde, blue-eyed, and wear pastel-coloured, lambswool jumpers. A 1980s American paperback uses a black and white photograph of a half-clothed woman in rather stylishly feminine versions of male clothing: a hat and waistcoated suit. The whole effect is slinky and sensual.

Virago Modern Classics all follow the same format of a painting, if possible by and always of women, framed in their standard green. For *The Well of Loneliness*, a painting by Gluck, the lesbian painter, is reproduced. It is called *Medallion* and shows two heads, cheek to cheek. The figures are androgynous women: short cropped hair, no make-up, noble features. This image represents lesbian whereas the others represent women; a subtle yet very obvious distinction. It also represents two women as lesbians, a way of underlining what most interpretations of the novel elide: that Mary is as much a lesbian as Stephen.

The Corgi paperback, which is possibly the most widely circulated version of *The Well of Loneliness*, has made some subtle changes. The novel has acquired a subtitle: The classic novel of lesbian love; and lost the preface by Havelock Ellis that the hardback editions contained from 1928 onwards. It has also lost its motto, from *Othello:* 'Nothing extenuate, Nor set down ought in malice'. The cover shows a chased picture frame within which is set the title and author and there is a barely discernible motto at the top of the frame: 'Friendship's sheltering tree'. The publisher's copy, on the reverse jacket speaks about the development of 'a natural tendency towards masculinity'; a description of lesbianism with which many would take issue.

Radclyffe Hall's treatment as a biographical subject is fascinating. There is no autobiographical writing, despite a popular misconception that *The Well of Loneliness* is her truth thinly disguised as fiction. While there are strong arguments for seeing the emotional and psychological truths of the novel as rooted in Radclyffe Hall's own belief system, it is neither accurate nor helpful to read *The Well of Loneliness* as an autobiographical piece of writing. What we know of Radclyffe

How does the Reader get on with Stephen Gordon?

Hall in terms of her life as a writer, a woman, and a lesbian has usually been refracted through the interests and, often, prejudices of others.

The first biography, *The Life and Death of Radclyffe Hall*, published in 1961, was written by Una, Lady Troubridge, her lover for over twenty years. It was followed in 1975 by Lovat Dickson's biography, *Radclyffe Hall at The Well of Loneliness: a Sapphic Chronicle*. 1984 saw the publication of Richard Ormrod's *Una Troubridge: The Friend of Radclyffe Hall*, and in 1985 Michael Baker's *Our Three Selves* was published. They are each quite different, although Dickson and Ormrod share something often found in male biographers of women writers that I can only liken to small boys peering up the skirts of women on buses. They do not understand anything, least of all their own prurient fascination with the subject. Una's biography both acknowledges and suffers from the limitations of her intimacy. It is difficult to imagine anyone attempting to extend the work of Michael Baker: his biography is exemplary.

There is a strong sense in *The Life and Death of Radclyffe Hall* that the writing has been forced on Una as a means of blocking other biographies. In settling to write it, Una is clear of the traps:

> An unexpurgated biography is of no value to anyone, an idealised biography would be an insult to her honesty and sincerity, but a perfectly truthful biography must of necessity involve others and include indiscretions of which she, with her high code of honour, might disapprove.
>
> (Troubridge, 1961: Foreword)

The account gives some detail about her early years but it does not seek to explain the adult woman through them and there is a sense of impatience. Una wants to get on to Radclyffe Hall the writer, not just because this includes the period of life they spent together, but because she believes this to have been Radclyffe Hall's destiny.

Radclyffe Hall's childhood was not typical and appears emotionally hard. She compensated for this in a number of ways: her fondness for animals and the vivid imagination through which she recast herself as a boy: Peter and then John,

How does the Reader get on with Stephen Gordon?

the name she took as an adult. Una points out that these traits, often taken as signs of sexual inversion, are very common in the development of girls. She sets down the various relationships Radclyffe Hall had with women, especially Ladye, who played an important role in turning her towards writing. She is open about the consequences of her affair and the effect upon their relationship of Ladye's death:

> at the time she continued chiefly for my sake, too numb with grief to feel any personal reaction, grew steadily and ripened between us until it became as precious, fulfilling and essential to her as ever it could be to me.
>
> (Troubridge, 1961: 55)

There then follows a narrative account of their life together: the involvement in spiritualism; Radclyffe's writing; travelling and friendships with the lesbian community in Paris; breeding dogs; and the various homes they lived in over the years. Una does not offer much in the way of analysis and it reads very one-dimensionally. What is important about the book, apart from setting out the facts and details of their lives, is that it takes for granted the fact of their relationship with each other. Such audacity is clearly, in the light of the *The Well of Loneliness* trial and their earlier, and in many ways much harder, skirmish with the Psychical Research Society, to be expected: they had nothing to hide and had proved that it was possible to survive such onslaughts. It is, however, important that they felt there was no need to apologize or to explain. Asked once by Ethel Mannin how as Catholics they dealt with confession, Una is reported to have been genuinely surprised by the question. To her mind there was no sin, no need for confession, and that sense of the right to their lives is a powerful message from the biography.

It would be too much, of course, to expect that right to be respected by future biographers. Lovat Dickson has written one of the most unpleasant books of biography it is possible to imagine. He had a tenuous connection with Radclyffe Hall and Una, as the friend of Harold Rubinstein, their lawyer, and through this was made co-executor of Una's will. He presents

How does the Reader get on with Stephen Gordon?

the writing of *Radclyffe Hall at The Well of Loneliness: a Sapphic Chronicle* as an enormous favour done to Una and the reading public. It is so riddled with such gross assumptions about lesbianism, it is almost funny. Except that these projections of misogynist and heterosexual fear are the only truth about lesbianism that many people ever recognize. Dickson has glimpsed Radclyffe Hall and Una in the cafes frequented by London society in 1929:

> they seemed alluring and attractive figures, and I wondered to myself, as young men do, what the heat of their strange passion did to those mask-like beautiful faces, those slender limbs, dressed now so oddly.
>
> (Dickson, 1975: 14)

> She had to control the aggressive instincts of the invert, ... the tragic element inseparable from the inverted nature. This love is barren.
>
> (Dickson, 1975: 229–30)

> We can sense the furious consuming passion, knowing climaxes and joys, some psychologists say, often beyond the experience of heterosexual lovers. Yet with its bitter aftertaste of barrenness.
>
> (Dickson, 1975: 22)

Throughout, Dickson refers to Mary Llewellyn as Mary Henderson. This is extremely sloppy writing and editing, but it is astonishing, given that the entire argument of *a Sapphic Chronicle* is that : 'The fictional form of the *The Well of Loneliness* is the thinnest of disguises' (Dickson, 1975: 9). He treats the beginning of the affair between Una and Radclyffe thus:

> Reading about this protracted wooing one is reminded of Stephen Gordon and Mary Henderson in *The Well of Loneliness*.... One cannot resist suspecting that the intensity of John's grief may in part have been a sexual ploy to entrap this young woman.
>
> (Dickson, 1975: 71)

The most consistent feeling that comes from this biography is an utter lack of respect for its subject. Dickson concludes that:

101

How does the Reader get on with Stephen Gordon?

> *The Well of Loneliness* is not just a cry of pain from the deprived
> abnormal, asking only to be understood; it tells the truth of what
> abnormal life is like, the dry aftertaste of passionate love when it
> cannot create, when it is sterile.
>
> (Dickson, 1975: 133)

Given that the novel underpins his entire sense of Radclyffe
Hall, it is hard for him to take a measured view of it and thus he
has little to offer the reader. It is interesting to compare Michael
Baker's approach to *The Well of Loneliness*, which appears to
take as its keynote Radclyffe Hall's own sense of what she was
doing by writing it.

> I have written a long and very serious novel entirely upon the
> subject of sexual inversion. So far as I know, nothing of the kind
> has ever been attempted before in fiction. Hitherto the subject
> has either been treated as pornography, or introduced as an
> episode. . . . I have treated it as a fact of nature.
>
> (Letter to her publishers quoted in Baker, 1985: 202)

Dickson's lack of respect is shown very clearly in the use he
makes of Compton Mackenzie's *Extraordinary Women*. That
Mackenzie's novel was never threatened with prosecution
makes it clear that biases were at work in the prosecution of *The
Well of Loneliness* connected with Hall's own lesbianism and
the book's refusal to mock or revile. Radclyffe Hall took
particular exception to *The Well of Loneliness* being used to
promote *Extraordinary Women* at a time when her book was
banned. Writing to her agent, Audrey Heath, in April 1929 she
threatened to sue, yet knew that: 'The case would be given
against me at once, because I would not deny being an invert. . . . Nothing that has gone before has hurt me like the
publication of *Extraordinary Women* in an ordinary edition'
(Quoted in Dickson, 1975: 180). The discrepancies here are
clearly of value and interest to a literary historian, but are lost
on Dickson, too much the victim of his own prejudices:

> They both deal with the same subject, lesbianism, but one does it
> wittily and with considerable literary skill, and the other with
> fanatical fierceness and a notable lack of humour. . . . How could

How does the Reader get on with Stephen Gordon?

such a witty young novelist resist a character like Radclyffe Hall,
the very caricature of the predatory lesbian.

(Dickson, 1975: 180–1)

By the end of *a Sapphic Chronicle*, it feels as if the depths
have been trawled, but no, Richard Ormrod in *Una Troubridge:
the Friend of Radclyffe Hall*, manages to sink further
still. Dickson has a curiously flirtatious relation to Una,
the contempt covered with a thin veneer of charm. With
Richard Ormrod such pretences are done away with. He is
derivative to an excessive degree, quoting wholesale from Una's
Life of Radclyffe Hall, all the while impressing upon us the
unreliability of her account. Inevitably, he uses *The Well of
Loneliness* as if it was unmediated autobiography. It is
interesting that he approaches Radclyffe Hall via Una, towards
whom he adopts a patronizing and proprietorial air. Una
described herself as the 'friend' of Radclyffe Hall, Ormrod finds
this inadequate: '"Wife", "consort", or even "lover" might be
more appropriate' (Ormrod, 1984: xvi). He cannot explain her
actions except by pathology; so we are told that she has an
unresolved electra complex and is: 'A basically hysterical
personality-type' (Ormrod, 1984: 18).

Much of the book is a straightforward rehashing of the detail
of their lives together as presented by Una in her own memoir;
Ormrod seems to see his role as filling in the motives behind
Una's actions, although those that could have been dwelt upon
profitably, notably the separation from Troubridge and the
question of custody and care of their daughter, Andrea, are
dealth with very summarily. What really bothers him is why
Una stayed with Radclyffe. At the point where Radclyffe
committed her life to writing, a commitment that by all
accounts was never easy for her, Una's role was encouraging,
supportive, and practical. Ormrod describes it thus: 'Una, ...
having a degree of natural masochism, enjoyed her role in this
exhaustive process. She was always happy in a supportive role'
(Ormrod, 1984: 151).

Apart from the rather insulting and sweeping dismissal of
Una's support, there is a denial of the active role that Una took

How does the Reader get on with Stephen Gordon?

in their relationship, primarily when they were both engaged in psychic research, but in literary respects, too. You would never know from reading this supposed biography of Una that she was a respected translator, responsible for bringing Colette to an English audience.

The real focus of this book, as with so many accounts of Radclyffe Hall and Una Troubridge's life together, is the trial of *The Well of Loneliness*. Ormrod sees it as important for literature, history, psychology, and within a history of censorship. For a biographer, he rather worryingly finds the novel: 'A rich source of information, inference, and perpetual question' (Ormrod, 1984: 167).

His own analysis of *The Well of Loneliness* is important in that it does make the distinction between Radclyffe Hall's own life and the book's overstatement of misery that was felt necessary in order to win sympathy. Ormrod ties himself up in knots trying to explain what an invert really is and does. He argues that its causes are both psychological and biological and that it is a state incompatible with being a woman. Using a rather deft argument, he ends by rescuing the book as a plea for tolerance towards transexualism, a rather novel way of disposing of its lesbian concerns and interest.

What is so valuable about *Our Three Selves*, (Baker, 1985), is that unlike the others it starts in a different place. It doesn't derive its structure nor its information from Una's account: instead, Michael Baker takes his own measure of Radclyffe Hall's life and achievments. The result is both an absorbing context for the writing, which is treated in some detail, and an account of the complexity of motives and relationships within which Radclyffe Hall lived. In terms of *The Well of Loneliness*, Michael Baker is interesting because he neither reduces her life to that moment, nor sees everything else that happens to her in relation to it. By decentring it in this way, and writing without prejudice, much more insight into the personal and literary character of Radclyffe Hall becomes possible.

Just as Radclyffe Hall has proved to be an interesting biographical subject, so has there been interest in writing about *The Well of Loneliness* itself. The first, and most unpleasant of

How does the Reader get on with Stephen Gordon?

these, was *The Sink of Solitude*, Beresford Egan's lampoon upon the trial, which was published in 1928. In blank verse and with a series of unpleasant drawings it proceeds to ruminate upon the novel and its prosecution.

> Romance is thus flung whop into the dirt
> And Stephen seeks to soothe her gaping hurt.
> Greyhounds are drawn to the electric hare
> The bus-conductor drawn towards the fare.
> Strong men at six are drawn towards the bar
> And gallery girls at stage doors seek the star.
> So all whom life has laid upon the mat
> Inevitably seeks a Chelsea-flat.
> To paint the chimneys or to write a book –
> The normal course abnormal STEPHEN took.

(Egan, 1928: 16)

The preface suggests a bullying anarchic freedom that holds sway against all petty restrictions and considerations. The lampoon is unkind to Joyson-Hicks and other small-minded censors, but far crueller to Radclyffe Hall:

> The pathetic post-war lesbians with their 'mannish' modes and poses; the sentimental scientificality of psychopaths like Havelock Ellis who ponderously explain them; the feebleness of *The Well of Loneliness* either as a work of art or as a moral argument.

(Egan, 1928: iv)

Vera Brittain, who had agreed to be a witness in the book's defence, wrote an account of the trial in 1968, perhaps in the wake of Lady Chatterley. The lesbianism is played down. The introduction by C. H. Rolph says: 'To its modern reader (are there any?) it would probably have no such air <of a personal crusade> if it were not for the now known personality of its author' (Brittain, 1968: 20). Apart from rendering invisible the lesbian reader, who has steadily provided a readership from 1928 onwards, the comment is odd coming in the very same year that Corgi's cheap paperback version was reprinted twice.

Little is added by this book to what we already know of the trial from Una's account. Vera Brittain is of the opinion that

How does the Reader get on with Stephen Gordon?

whereas lesbianism at the time of the trial was: 'classified as sin, wanton and unashamed' it would now be seen to: 'Lay in glandular abnormalities' (Brittain, 1968: 60). And Vera Brittain sees it as a source of regret that Radclyffe Hall was: 'Now inescapably the author of *The Well of Loneliness* and seemed unlikely to avoid her unjust fate of exclusive identification with the lesbian world' (Brittain, 1968: 83).

Vera Brittain is less restrained than Una Troubridge about opposition to *The Well of Loneliness*. She quotes, approvingly from Egan:

> But for the combined efforts of James Douglas and Joynson-Hicks, the book would more than probably have fallen into insignificance already. ... Thanks to their crusade, millions of shop, office and millgirls have been led to ask the furtive question: What is lesbianism?
>
> (quoted in Brittain, 1968: 97–8)

Drawing on transcripts and other documentation from the attempted prosecution in America, Vera Brittain makes it quite clear that the most antagonistic feature of *The Well of Loneliness* was Hall's refusal to make her characters apologetic for what they were or did.

Jane Rule, in *Lesbian Images*, published in 1975, devotes a chapter to Radclyffe Hall and *The Well of Loneliness*, which she discusses in relation to Bloomsbury's openness about sexuality. The influence of *The Well of Loneliness* is acknowledged, but she is critical of the medical models it perpetuates and the way it devalues women's experience.

> *Loneliness* is an important book because it does so carefully reveal the honest misconceptions about women's nature and experience which have limited and crippled so many people. ... She worshipped the very institutions which oppressed her, the Church and the patriarchy, which have taught women there are only two choices, inferiority or perversion. Inside that framework, she made and tried to redefine the only proud choice she had. The 'bible' she offered is really no better for women than the Bible she would not reject.
>
> (Rule, 1975: 61)

How does the Reader get on with Stephen Gordon?

Radclyffe Hall hasn't interested contemporary critics concerned with traditions of women's writing. The field of enquiry drawn up in the mid 1970s excludes lesbians from feminism. Hall is mentioned in the bibliography of Ellen Moers' *Literary Women* as a writer of novels and Elaine Showalter's *A Literature of Their Own* discusses *The Unlit Lamp* as a novel about expectations put upon women. Her biographical listing simply refers to *The Well of Loneliness* as Radclyffe Hall's best known work.

It isn't until the 1980s and the beginnings of lesbian studies as a distinct area of enquiry that Radclyffe Hall comes under scrutiny from lesbian feminist critics. The first of these is Lillian Faderman, whose exhaustive account of lesbian themes in the history of women's writing, *Surpassing The Love of Men*, devotes a whole chapter to Radclyffe Hall and *The Well of Loneliness*. Faderman (1981) is very critical of the novel, seeing Hall as an apologist for dubious medical ideas about lesbian existence. Her arguments have a great deal of truth, but at the same time her view of *The Well of Loneliness* is somewhat partial. Although Faderman is taking a historical perspective in her study, there are times when it appears curiously ahistorical: there is a strong sense that Hall is being criticized for not thinking ahead of her times and is personally responsible for the negative use to which her novel has been put by a homophobic culture:

> It was widely used in college abnormal psychology classes, and was the only lesbian novel known to the masses. But many lesbians who read the book during Hall's day and after felt angered and betrayed by it. An American sociological study of lesbians in the 1920s and 1930s indicated that 'almost to a woman, they decried its publication.' They believed that if the novel did not actually do harm to their cause, at the least it 'put homosexuality in the wrong light.'... it plays a sad, prominent part in many an individual lesbian history ... its writer fell into the congenitalist trap ... morbidifies the most natural impulses and healthy views. It reinforced the notion that some women would not marry not because the institution was unjust, that they sought independence, not because they believed it would make them whole people, that they loved other women not

How does the Reader get on with Stephen Gordon?

because such love was natural - but instead because they were born into the wrong body.

(Faderman, 1981: 322–3)

Throughout the early 1980s *The Well of Loneliness* was discussed in the context of developing lesbian and feminist studies. *Signs: The Lesbian Issue* and *Lesbian Studies*, two American journals, each included an essay on Radclyffe Hall. Toni A. H. McNaron in *Lesbian Studies* contributes an interesting essay entitled 'A journey into otherness: teaching *The Well of Loneliness*' in which she discusses having assigned the novel as part of a Women's Studies course concerned with 'otherness'. She charts a process whereby each member of the group became separated off from the others: how the book divided the class by emphasizing a sense of otherness:

> Lesbianism was the only topic that affected us in this way. . . . We had each participated in making the lesbian into our own special other or in making ourselves as lesbianism into everyone else's other. We had oppressed and divided ourselves.
>
> (McNaron, 1982: 90)

Here they were finally able to see from what need to defend their own choices and sense of themselves – as heterosexual feminists, lesbian feminists, teachers, etc. – they spoke and used the experience positively:

> We were willing to suspend content and descend into the more frightening and liberating fears of process and feeling. I also believe it was no accident that it was a novel focusing on lesbian reality which precipitated the journey. . . . To bring those unspeakable, formerly even unnameable responses up and out into the open, especially within a classroom setting, is to put us in touch with our own self-repressions.
>
> (McNaron, 1982: 92)

Esther Newton's 1985 essay 'The mythic mannish lesbian: Radclyffe Hall and the new woman' in *Signs: The Lesbian Issue* is an important piece of work. It confronts directly the difficulty presented to contemporary lesbian feminist readers by *The Well of Loneliness*:

How does the Reader get on with Stephen Gordon?

Unable to wish Radclyffe Hall away, sometimes even hoping to reclaim her, our feminist scholars have lectured, excused, or patronised her. Radclyffe Hall, they declare, was an unwitting dupe of the misogynist doctors' attack on feminist romantic friendship. Or, cursed with a pessimistic temperament and brainwashed by Catholicism, Hall parroted society's condemnation of lesbians. The 'real' Radclyffe Hall lesbian novel, this argument frequently continues, the one that ought to have been famous, is her first, *The Unlit Lamp* (1924). Better yet, Virginia Woolf's *Orlando* (1928) should have been the definitive lesbian novel. Or Natalie Barney's work, or anything but *The Well*.

Heterosexual conservatives condemn *The Well* for defending the lesbian's right to exist; lesbian feminists condemn it for presenting lesbians as different from women in general. But *The Well* has continuing meaning to lesbians because it confronts the stigma of lesbianism – as most lesbians have had to live it. Maybe Natalie Barney with her fortune and her cast-iron ego, or safely married Virginia Woolf were able to pooh-pooh the patriarchy, but most lesbians have had to face being called or at least feeling like freaks. As the Bowery bum represents all that is most feared and despised about drunkenness, the mannish lesbian, of whom Stephen Gordon is the most famous prototype, has symbolised the stigma of lesbianism and so continues to move a broad range of lesbians.

(Newton, 1985: 9–10)

What is most powerful about this essay is the way in which it acknowledges the very real difficulties contemporary readers have with *The Well of Loneliness*, while at the same time using historical knowledge about forms of femininity, feminism, and lesbianism to explain, but not excuse, the choices available to and made by Radclyffe Hall in her life and writing.

Hall's association of lesbianism and masculinity needs to be challenged not because it doesn't exist, but because it is not the only possibility. Gender identity and sexual preference are, in fact, two related but separate systems; witness the profusion of gender orientations (which are deeply embedded in race, class, and ethnic experience) to be found in the lesbian community. Many lesbians are masculine; most have composite styles; many are emphatically feminine. Stephen Gordon's success eclipsed more esoteric, continental, and feminine images of the lesbian such as Renée Vivien's decadent or Colette's bisexual. The notion of a feminine lesbian contradicted the congenital theory

How does the Reader get on with Stephen Gordon?

that many homosexuals in Hall's era espoused to counter-demands that they undergo punishing 'therapies'.

(Newton, 1985: 25)

A similarly useful analysis is that developed by Sonja Ruehl in her essay 'Inverts and experts: Radclyffe Hall and the lesbian identity', which was published in 1982 as part of a collection of essays on *Feminism, Culture and Politics,* (Brunt and Rowan, 1982). Sonja Ruehl uses ideas developed in Foucault's analysis of sexuality in order to argue that *The Well of Loneliness* constructs a reverse discourse about lesbianism, one that contests the existing categorizations. It does this because Radclyffe Hall in *The Well of Loneliness,* for the first time, speaks of lesbianism, not as a medico-psychology expert or as a moral guardian, but as a lesbian. Thus the naming of lesbianism as either sin or sickness is done alongside an experience of it, which must address the: 'social consequences of a lesbian identity and to explore, not only sexual relationships, but those involving family and friends' (Ruehl, 1982: 20–1).

In discussing the novel, she dwells on Stephen's innocence and the ways in which the class relations are used to generate a fictional matrix of conventional romance, but her main concern is with how Radclyffe Hall has utilized the writings of the sexologists, especially Havelock Ellis. She charts the ways in which Hall adopts a far more rigid definition of lesbianism than Havelock Ellis did, but argues that this polarity makes it more provocative and that this is more suited to a public arena. She concludes that by shifting lesbianism from the individual to the social scale, making: 'Inversion ... a problem for society to face and not just a moral dilemma for 'inverted' individuals' (Ruehl, 1982: 28) the novel becomes of major importance in defining lesbian identity.

A similar set of ideas are developed and expanded by Jean Radford in her essay, 'An inverted romance: *The Well of Loneliness* and sexual ideology'. There, she acknowledges the influences between Hall's writing and the sexologists and expands our understanding of the novel by looking at what features it shares with heterosexual romance.

How does the Reader get on with Stephen Gordon?

> In Radclyffe Hall's inverted romance, the heroine becomes a 'hero' by renouncing the love of a woman: the invert renounces an individual love relationship in the name of the 'suffering millions' of women and men for whom the novel speaks.
>
> (Radford, 1986: 110)

The only full-length literary critical study of Radclyffe Hall is that written by Claudia Stillman Franks in 1982, *Beyond The Well of Loneliness*. Her project is important, though ambiguous, rooted as it is in a desire to rescue Hall from her lesbianism and her biographers: 'To discuss her as a writer of talent, one whose books are still worth reading today, rather than as part of a particular movement' (Franks, 1982: x).

Her argument is that the themes of Hall's writing are consistent across all the novels and that they share a concern with: 'Quest, or of the struggle of the characters to attune themselves simultaneously to their inner needs and to the demands the world makes upon them' (Franks, 1982: 6). In her biographical discussion of Radclyffe Hall, she relies heavily and uncritically upon Lovat Dickson but adds an original dimension by charting connections between Radclyffe Hall and other women writers: Rebecca West, May Sinclair, I.A.R. Wylie, and Violet Hunt. Franks places Radclyffe Hall in relation to other writers and movements in writing, something that a too narrow focus on *The Well of Loneliness* has obscured:

> her writing reflects a body of concerns which was fairly typical of the Georgian psychological novel. Unlike the great and self-proclaimed experimentalists (Joyce, Woolf, D.H. Lawrence), she was one of many authors who were more quietly introducing psychological themes into the mainstream of English fiction.
>
> (Franks, 1982: 38)

Her reading of *The Well of Loneliness* is unusual in that she sees it as a book about the process of becoming a writer:

> Stephen Gordon's character and fate are, to some extent determined not only by her psychosexual orientation, but also by her aesthetic temperament and by her artists' sensibility. *The*

How does the Reader get on with Stephen Gordon?

> *Well of Loneliness* is paradoxically both dated and universal – dated in its psychological assumptions, but universal in its analysis of a writer's aspirations and limitations. ... I do not mean to deny the thematic centrality of her lesbianism .... Concerning the issue of Stephen's lesbianism, there is really little to say ... however, there is much to say about her treatment of imagination.
>
> (Franks, 1982: 98)

Franks is at times a little too quick to dispose of lesbianism, seeing in *The Unlit Lamp*, for instance, themes: 'rich enough to deserve portrayal without the added complication of the lesbian co-plot' (Franks, 1982: 52), but her observations about how rarely women's careers as artists are publicly discussed are important and the value of reading Hall's work from that perspective are valuable. She makes an interesting point about the ways in which both Sir Philip and Puddle encourage Stephen to link her writing with her sexuality:

> From the beginning though the act of authorship for Stephen is not merely a means of expressing herself spontaneously and creatively; it is also both a compensation for her earliest feelings of alienation and a means of mastering aspects of her personality which she cannot fully understand or integrate.
>
> (Franks, 1982: 104)

What begins for Stephen as liberating, ultimately becomes negative when writing has to compensate for the suffering caused by her sexuality. For Stephen, 'Success or failure with individual novels, and her attitude towards her writing in general, is a direct function of her view of herself as a lesbian in society at any given stage in her career' (Franks, 1982: 114).

This is a challenging argument, though not fully developed because it does not acknowledge how central questions of sexual identity, and the security to write from them, are. The question here is not either/or, as regards lesbianism and writing, but how to articulate the two together.

In seeing Radclyffe Hall's work as basically about artistic development and integrity, Claudia Stillman Franks is able to bring Stephen Gordon into the mainstream of her writerly concerns:

How does the Reader get on with Stephen Gordon?

Stephen Gordon, then, is far from an unusual character in the Radclyffe Hall canon, and, although the problems she faces as a lesbian in society are painfully real, I do not think it an exaggeration to say that her lesbianism also serves as a type of metaphor for the alienation that Radclyffe Hall saw at the root of human existence.

(Franks, 1982: 162)

In general, then, the critical work on Radclyffe Hall and *The Well of Loneliness* has been patchy. Claudia Stillman Franks' work establishes a framework for discussion which, when taken with a more focused lesbian analysis of her work, gives back to Radclyffe Hall the integrity and respect denied her by most of her biographers.

Chapter Five

WHO READS *THE WELL OF LONELINESS*?

THE IMPLIED preferred reader of *The Well of Loneliness* is heterosexual. It is a book written to explain lesbianism: to generate sympathy, tolerance, and understanding. As a book that has sold millions of copies, it is reasonable to assume that a large proportion of its readership, certainly initially, was drawn from heterosexuals. To what extent did it succeed in changing public opinion?

Shifts of that order are never caused by one incident alone, though such events can condense and focus other changes. One of the most significant contributions *The Well of Loneliness* made was to render lesbianism visible. Some previous knowledge was there, for lesbians and for others: Una had left her husband, Admiral Troubridge, for Radclyffe Hall; Vita Sackville West and Violet Trefusis had eloped to France together, and the movement of women towards each other, was happening, had happened, in countless lives of the less newsworthy. What there had not been was the publicity of scandal. When, with the trial, this happened, the degree of vitriol and antagonism towards lesbians was unmistakable. Alongside all who found this a proper response to immorality, there will have been others questioning such bigotry.

By the late 1960s, when a more tolerant attitude towards homosexuality and sexuality in general was evident, the preface to an account of the trial of *The Well of Loneliness* confidently assumes that the book has no contemporary readers. The assumption is not just that there are no lesbian readers for

114

Who reads The Well of Loneliness?

whom the novel would have continuing interest, but that heterosexual readers, in the absence of an immediate scandal, would have no cause to read it either. The attraction of *The Well of Loneliness* for a good few of its heterosexual readers would have been less a desire to understand and sympathize with the plight of lesbians than a search for voyeuristic titillation, often encouraged by the book's paperback presentation. Comparing *The Well of Loneliness* with soft-porn novels of the 1960s, it is likely that their disappointment in the novel left it part-read.

But there will always be heterosexual readers who genuinely want to know more about lesbian life: parents of lesbian children, partners who have been left for another woman, friends of women coming out, and women starting to question their own sexuality. The publicity surrounding *The Well of Loneliness* ensures its place within the cultural map as *the* novel about lesbian life: the one novel everyone has heard about. Whenever knowledge of lesbianism is wanted, for whatever reasons, it will be to *The Well of Loneliness* that people turn. This tagging of the name is further enhanced by the fact that of lesbian writing, it is likely to be the most accessible: published in a cheap, mass-marketed format, available from W. H. Smith, on the library shelf. Certainly, until within the last five or ten years, when some bookshops started to categorize and display lesbian and gay books separately and the recent highly commendable development of lesbian and gay sections in some libraries, people simply would not have known where or what to look for other than *The Well of Loneliness*.

These readers have particular reasons for reading about lesbianism. They come wanting to know how their child, or their friend might live: wanting to know what it means to be a lesbian. Attitudes to lesbianism often exist in society and ideology independently of any knowledge of how lesbians actually live and explain their lives to themselves. The common conception is of lesbianism as a phase, an immaturity, which can become fixed as a negative state: sick and sorry; decadent; ugly; the consequences of failing the demands of hetero-

Who reads The Well of Loneliness?

sexuality. *The Well of Loneliness* seems to have been more powerful in fixing an image of what a lesbian is rather than in arguing against prejudice. What is unfortunate for lesbians is that this image is itself a distortion that becomes one of the worst stereotypes.

Perhaps more damaging than the figure of a lesbian that it generates, is the removal of lesbianism from anything that approximates to everyday life. *The Well of Loneliness* is a romance, and as such, is stylized and unnaturalistic. However, there are moments in the text that are clearly documentary in approach and strive for a realist effect. The clearest example of this is in Radclyffe Hall's account of the Parisian bars and their lesbian culture. She is deliberately striving for authority as a chronicler of these times, as someone who describes and explains lesbians to people who would not otherwise encounter them. The romance presentation of British culture and the realistic presentation of Paris: a place that is removed physically as well as imaginatively means lesbianism is taken away from the places most lives are lived.

The ways *The Well of Loneliness* formed heterosexual readers' expectations of what it is to be a lesbian are serious, but less so than the effects of the novel on lesbian readers. For many years it was a bible for lesbians: a source book for behaviour, attitude, and dress; a salve for the hurts of the world; an inspiration and example. Now, with more lesbian writing and a more politicized context for lesbian lives, its role in defining lesbianism has shifted, but its power is still substantial.

A reliable index of its power is how often it is referenced elsewhere in the culture. There are many instances in fiction and real life of significant offerings of *The Well of Loneliness*: to recommend the book is to make a statement about yourself and the woman to whom your are recommending it. Many women pinpoint their realization that *The Well of Loneliness* existed in reading some lesbian subplot where it is referred to. It has also been reclaimed by the lesbian culture in other ways. Cath Jackson's cartoons ran for weeks in *City Limits*, relying almost entirely for their effect upon a knowledge of *The Well of Loneliness* and its importance for lesbians.

Who reads The Well of Loneliness?

Such irreverence is only possible where understandings are shared and secure and were taken to a new extreme by the theatre group Hard Corps whose play *John*, performed in 1985, began life as an idea for doing:

> a musical of *The Well of Loneliness*. Everyone thought it was a wonderful idea. I fantasised about chorus lines of Radclyffe Halls in green smoking jackets kicking their legs across the room and lines of girls in dressing gowns reading *The Well of Loneliness* under the covers.
>
> (*Women's Review*, 4 February 1986)

Explaining their decision to focus on Radclyffe Hall and then, later, on Natalie Barney's circle they say: 'Let's do preposterous women! We'd had an overdose of honest, well-meaning, good women' (Women's Review, 4 February 1986).

The play was a great success, especially with lesbians, but it seems to me no coincidence that the idea and its execution, as well as the comment about 'preposterous women' comes from Adele Saleem, a woman who is not a lesbian. For lesbians, the question of Radclyffe Hall: the non-feminist foremother is usually more complicated.

Recently, in the light of Clause 28, women who criticized Radclyffe Hall and *The Well of Loneliness* out of hand are reconsidering their opinion. Whereas previously they saw and rejected in the novel unequal and role-ridden relationships between women, they now pick up on the defiance: the articulation and opposition to bigotry and prejudice.

READERSHIP SURVEYS OF *THE WELL OF LONELINESS*

For this section of the chapter, I am drawing upon responses to questionnaires on *The Well of Loneliness*. One was carried out by a lesbian archive in America; the other I drew up and distributed myself. This was done before the attack on lesbian and gay civil liberties, which Clause 28 represents. If repeated now, I think opinions about Radclyffe Hall would have shifted.

Who reads The Well of Loneliness?

America

The New York-based Lesbian Herstory Archives launched its series of cultural surveys in 1986 with *The Well of Loneliness*. Their aim was to: 'Attempt to understand how we use and judge our own cultural roots.' The questions they asked were about: age at which the book was read and age of coming out; how and what had been heard of the novel and how a copy was found; reactions to the book: whether there were characters to identify with or feel strongly about, either negatively or postively; whether the book was discussed with other people; whether on rereading, opinions changed; and finally, whether this had been the first lesbian book read and if not, what was.

Over 150 women responded to their survey and they reviewed 100 to chart basic demographic facts. They found that the most frequent age-of-reading was 20. The youngest age was 10, by a woman who came out twenty-six years later and the oldest age-of-reading was 40, reported both by a woman who had come out 22 years earlier and by a woman who came out at the same time as she read the book. All three of these women reported a postive response. About one-third of their respondents came out in Brooklyn or New York City and they refer to a wide variety of other locations including: Helsinki, Berlin, Salt Lake City, and boarding school. As my questions were framed somewhat differently, I will reproduce some of the responses from America directly. Their interest was in the book generally, whereas my survey concentrated more on the character of Stephen Gordon and was trying to gauge how far there was both an awareness of the book and of the author's reputation.

The American survey picks up a wider historical spread of readings, with comments from women who read it in the 1930s, 40s and 50s; and there are interesting accounts of how copies were found. They don't say whether the consensus was positive or not, but they extract fairly positive accounts for the sample they reproduce. It is possible to see the perpetuation of negative images and expectations, but also to detect the ways in which women have used the book positively:

Who reads The Well of Loneliness?

My mother gave it me to read on a long bus ride. She said it was the first book about lesbians. I still don't fully understand her motivation.

(Read in 1959, aged 14)

In 1930 – I was at school in Paris, but extremely shy. I did manage to get myself to Adrienne Monnier's bookshop – circled timidly about, browsing – but could not find the courage to request the book ... in the first year of my married life, and pregnant, I came upon a copy – without even looking for it – in the within-walking-distance Public Library.

(Read in 1930, aged 19)

Right now I am without a copy – have passed on many – but have reread it more than once and am always moved by Rad. Hall's courage as by the dear book itself.

(Read in 1930, aged 19)

Discuss it with people? No! What other people? All the other lesbians were in Europe.

(Read in 1938, aged 18)

The most important things were 1) simply that the book existed and 2) it suggested that somewhere I might find a community, if only a small and beleagured one – someday.

(Read in 1946, aged 15)

Even though I am 'Feminine' in appearance I identified with Stephen and admire her. The ending of the novel dismayed me so that I rewrote it.

(Read in 1970, aged 13)

The book is a real downer. It was the first time I had cried, really cried from a story. I guess I had 'read' in it that was what was in store for all of us in our future. I was crying for myself. ... The reason I reacted to the book as I did is probably because I feel that society hasn't changed a damn bit and never will. We will always be misfits and outsiders in their eyes. The only change possible is in how we feel about ourselves and what we do to change our position in society, i.e. political change.

(Read in 1970, aged 21)

Who reads The Well of Loneliness?

Britain and Ireland

My own survey was done through a combination of personal contacts, advertising, and circulating lesbian educational and cultural events. For this reason there is a bias towards London, 74 per cent in the 40 questionnaires that were returned. The majority of respondents were middle class: 60 per cent as opposed to 10 per cent who defined themselves as upper class and 30 per cent working class. The racial breakdown showed 57.5 per cent as White British, 12.5 per cent Jewish, 7.5 per cent European, 7.5 per cent American, 5 per cent Afro-Caribbean, 5 per cent Celtic, and 5 per cent Australian. A number of women commented on being asked these questions. Some by pointing to the difficulty involved in answering, where for example they had working-class parents but had received higher education themselves or where there was a complex racial background. Others simply commented on the irrelevance or cheek of the question: 'What a question!!' and 'What's the point of this?'

The majority of women taking part in the survey were between 36 and 45 years of age, the most frequent age of reading was 24 with the youngest aged 13 and the oldest aged 40. The highest percentage of readers were divided equally between those who read the book under the age of 21 and those who had read it between the ages of 21 and 28. This accounted for 74 per cent of all the readings. Although I had not asked a specific question about coming out, it was possible to establish in some cases when the book had been read in relation to coming out. The spread was almost equal: 50 per cent had read it after coming out; 46 per cent during that process, and only 4 per cent while still identifying as heterosexual women.

What was known of the novel in advance

Although I did not ask directly whether women had had a positive or negative reaction to the book, it was possible to draw that out. I had asked about opinions changing on rereading. These comments proved illuminating both of the ways in which expectations and therefore opinions of a book like *The Well of Loneliness* do change, but also of the ways in which

Who reads The Well of Loneliness?

women are determined to make positive readings from what appears at first sight to be a fairly bleak novel. There were slightly more positive reactions than negative, 54 per cent as opposed to 38 per cent, with a further 8 per cent where it was not possible to judge. Of these, 61.5 per cent had reread the novel at some point and of these 40 per cent had not changed their opinion of the novel at all. The others however, had, with 20 per cent finding their initially positive reaction qualified and 40 per cent finding a negative response transformed into something more positive. These figures surprised me. I had expected them to be reversed and it indicates, I think, the complex of needs that make up the criteria through which we assess the value of lesbian writing. It was also interesting to find that women who had not read the novel understood it was an unhappy novel: 'It doesn't paint a happy picture of us lesbians' (Not read: aged 25).

This was also evident in replies to the question I had asked about what women knew of the novel before they read it:

> I'd known of it for ages. I'd heard of the trial, knew that it was a lesbian novel and had heard it was a negative portrayal of lesbians ....I didn't find it as negative as expected, especially the portrayal of other women.
>
> (Read in 1987, aged 25)

> It was mentioned in one of the books about women's narrative I was reading at University ... quite outdated and melodramatic – I remember this comment ... but when I read it the first time I was very involved, and I enjoyed it (I cried a lot).... It is melodramatic (boring sometimes), but I'm still very fond of it. Parts of it are great like that about the two women's holiday in Spain – parts a bit ridiculous.
>
> (Read in 1979, aged 19)

Perhaps here, in balancing what they have heard about the book with their own reactions to it, we can see most clearly the ways in which lesbians reading *The Well of Loneliness* maximize the book's potential. Responses such as the following demonstrate an intelligent and very critical reading:

Who reads The Well of Loneliness?

I had heard a lot of discussion about how awful it was; had been some of my friends' first contact with lesbianism and had revolted/scared them. Women laughed about it a lot or seemed quite critical of Radclyffe Hall for writing it. However her bravery was also recognised and it was seen as a lesbian classic. I do not wish to mock her. I now see this book as a useful example of what happens when lesbians present themselves in ways to maximise acceptance in any given historical/social context. The book is addressed to heterosexuals. It is a plea for toleration on their terms. Radclyffe Hall did not feel she could afford in this book to represent more positive or challenging images. ... We are all still engaged in presenting accounts of lesbianism whether in books or conversations. It is important to think about what image we are presenting and why.

(Read in 1980, aged 18)

Hated the ending but loved the book. But still *The Well* is so willing to deal with lesbians as complex and intricate beings which so few lesbian books do.

(Read in 1984, aged 33)

For many women, though, the reconsideration of Radclyffe Hall comes, if it comes at all, after they have fully experienced the negative impact of the novel:

I knew it was a lesbian novel and banned for 'obscenity'. Lesbian yes, obscene – no – I did not like the insistence that Stephen was a man in all but body. I loathed it.

(Read in 1975, aged 20)

When I was nineteen I wasn't able to finish it, I think the prose style and class assumptions put me off. Had I finished reading the novel then I think it would have been very harmful, it would have added to the feelings of 'queerness' and doom that were already well-established in me. ... I think I had some notion of it being 'the' lesbian novel. I now see it as a novel written by a lesbian as an apology to heterosexuals, which unfortunately is seen by many lesbians as a novel for and about us.

(Read in 1968, aged 19 and in 1981, aged 32)

I didn't quite know whether Radclyffe Hall was male or female.

(Read in 1971, aged 18)

I had read the novel which mentions *The Well of Loneliness* more than once in its pages and so I became curious. ... it was

Who reads The Well of Loneliness?

really good but it really depressed me and sort of made me bitter and want to turn against all those against the 'homo' society. It was useful in that it made me realise I am not the only one passing through all the unfair treatment of the 'world' towards lesbians. Harmful in that the end seems to make one think there is little hope for the homosexual.

(Read in 1987, aged 23)

Positive reactions to the novel often include an awareness of the factors that make the novel appear negative:

Have read it several times, find it moving, exasperating, and melodramatic, but it also tugs at something in me: it's an important book.

(Read in 1974, aged 25)

and other reactions are less qualified:

I knew little about other lesbians and it made me feel less lonely. I found the book well written and I enjoyed it as a novel *per se*.

(Read in 1955, aged 26)

At the time I found it wonderful and I think the romance was useful, uplifting, showed the possibility of lesbiansim – But I didn't want to be a martyr, live in a twilight world. . . . But it did give me a sense of a cause which did actually spur me a bit.

(Read in 1964, aged 14)

Did opinions change on rereading?

The majority of women had reread and subsequently revised their opinions of the novel. These make very interesting reading, showing the variability in interpretations of the novel itself, as well as readers' particular, and changing, needs.

At 17 I was prepared to be cynical about it, but I was also much more involved with the story than I had expected to be. Now I'm as cynical as ever about Hall as a writer, but have to admire her courage.

(Read in 1965, aged 17)

At first I thought it was wonderful, although depressing, because it was the first account of lesbianism I'd read. Now I think it is

Who reads The Well of Loneliness?

not one of Radclyffe Hall's best novels and that it is negative and
too heavily based on the sexologists views of lesbianism.
(Read in 1981, aged 24)

A number of women made the point that the context in which
we read novels needs to be clearer. Most women came to *The
Well of Loneliness* through rumour and suggestions, a source
of knowledge that was often inaccurate. A sequence of
questions and answers points this up to comic effect:

I knew it was famous, banned, and hard to find.
Q. Was this accurate? A. Not Really ...
Q. Where did you get your copy from? A. The Library.
(Read in 1965, aged 17)

But for many women the consequences were more serious:

Most of what I was reading was essentially negative (in 1967–8
most of what was written was!) but I was struggling to find my
own identity regardless. I reread it twice. Once about 10 years
ago after I'd accepted my sexuality, when I found it essentially
negative and depressive and much more recently in the Virago
edition, where I found Alison Hennegan's introduction very
useful and interesting. At this point I found it much more
interesting as part of our 'literary heritage'.
(Read in 1965, aged 20)

WAS IT THE FIRST LESBIAN NOVEL READ?

Given the notoriety of *The Well of Loneliness*, it was surprising
to find that it was the first lesbian novel to be read by only 37
per cent of women. Those women who had read other books
first and noted them, demonstrated quite a wide variety of
novels and sociological accounts: pulp New English Library
novels; Colette's *Claudine Married*; *Orlando* by Virginia Woolf;
La Bâtarde by Violette Leduc; *Rubyfruit Jungle* by Rita Mae
Brown; *Sister Gin* by June Arnold; *Patience and Sarah* by Isobel
Miller; and *The Microcosm* by Maureen Duffy.

Who reads The Well of Loneliness?

Other books by Radclyffe Hall that had been read

I wanted to see whether women had read just *The Well of Loneliness* or other works by Radclyffe Hall and if so, what they though of them. The split was almost equal: 56 per cent had read other works by Radclyffe Hall, 44 per cent had not. Of those other works, by far the most common was *The Unlit Lamp*: 60 per cent had read that and 28 per cent had read some or all of her other novels. Only one woman had read her poems, a woman who had in fact privately reprinted her most explicitly lesbian poetry: 'A Sheaf of Verses', in 1985. Interestingly, although she was the only woman to mention the poems, two other women, enthusiasts for Radclyffe Hall's work, described themselves as having read 'everything;' and 'the lot'.

For some women, reading other works by Radclyffe Hall just confirms their original negative impression:

> Not so frightening! Equally badly written.
>
> (Read in 1962, aged 16)

There are also those readers for whom it is a means of forming an opinion about Hall's work generally:

> [she] was a committed writer about 'outsiders'.
>
> (Read in 1953, aged 27)

> It shows a more interesting side of Radclyffe Hall.
>
> (Read in 1982, aged 40)

In terms of opinions about her other work, the most illuminating comments concern comparisons between *The Well of Loneliness* and *The Unlit Lamp* and the ways in which reading for lesbianism is a definite and legitimate demand made of books:

> Literary better, subject matter not as interesting obviously.
>
> (Read in 1971, aged 18)

> I don't much like her writing so Well of Loneliness was only relevant for theme.
>
> (Read in 1965, aged 20)

Who reads The Well of Loneliness?

Boring - not lesbian!

(Read in 1965, aged 17)

Good stories but not about lesbians.

(Read in 1972, aged 25)

The relationship between *The Well of Loneliness* and *The Unlit Lamp* is interesting. Women recognize the heavy handedness of *The Well of Loneliness* and find the *The Unlit Lamp* more plausible and engaging to read. Free of her didacticism, Hall can concentrate more on the precision of character and motivation. At the same time, though, the inexplicitness of *The Unlit Lamp* is not quite enough. Lesbianism is socially invisible, therefore a degree of didacticism is required:

> *The Unlit Lamp* seems to have more psychological truth and certainly to be much more relevant to modern lesbian feminism than *The Well*.
>
> (Read in 1968, aged 19)

> *Much* better written but the explicitness of *The Well of Loneliness* is important.
>
> (Read in 1974, aged 25)

> *The Unlit Lamp* is a less clichéd piece of writing – i.e. no het. romances, etc. and very moving and depressing – more so than *The Well*, I think.
>
> (Read in 1981, aged 33)

> *The Unlit Lamp* is much better as a novel. Not explicitly lesbian – subtlety works better. Equally or more tragic than *The Well* but in a more palatable way.
>
> (Read in 1982, aged 22)

> *The Unlit Lamp* is completely different, apart from the theme of love between pupil and governess, which is not developed in *The Well*. It is the story of a Stephen who gives up – probably sadder than The Well.
>
> (Read in 1979, aged 19)

Who reads The Well of Loneliness?

WOULD YOU RECOMMEND THE NOVEL?

Because so many lesbians come to read *The Well of Loneliness* on the recommendation of, usually, other lesbians, I was interested to see whether women had or would ever recommend the book and with what reservations. The significance of the answers lay in the nature of reservations women identified and also because of the distinctions within the reading public they made. Women were very conscious of the differences between younger and older lesbians; between lesbians and straights; between women coming out and those more secure in their lesbian identities. Only 15 per cent would never recommend the book to anyone.

> Never! Never! Never! While there is so much better contemporary lesbian writing and lesbian writing emerging from the same period as *The Well of Loneliness*.
> (Read in 1953, aged 27)

> No. I consider this book very bad news for lesbians.
> (Read in 1962, aged 16)

Of the rest, 45 per cent would recommend the novel and this included women who seemed to find the question ridiculous, so sure were they of the book's value.

> Yes of course I would
> (Read in 1976, aged 22)

> Yes, definitely, I have, and will. I think that it is a classic of lesbian literature and history.
> (Read in 1979, aged 19)

> Yes, if only to appreciate Radclyffe Hall's own particular struggle.
> (Read in 1971, aged 18)

and there was, finally, the rather ambiguous recommendation:

> Yes, though not as a lesbian novel.
> (Read in 1987, aged 20)

Who reads The Well of Loneliness?

The 40 per cent who would recommend with reservation were divided into two main categories: those for whom their reserve was about who should read it and when; and those who saw it as an important historical document but in no way representative of lesbian life as such.

Some women were concerned that the book shouldn't be read by heterosexual people:

> Yes, but not straights.
>
> (Read in 1975, aged 20)

> I would recommend it to an 'out' dyke but not to a heterosexual woman or an emerging lesbian.
>
> (Read in 1981, aged 24)

Young women and emerging lesbians preoccupied a lot of women:

> Not as a first, personally I experienced it as a very negative view, especially with the introduction going on about 'inverts'.
>
> (Read in 1980, aged 34)

> Not isolated lesbian teenagers – women don't need to be men, transvestites, etc. to love women sexually.
>
> (Read in 1964, aged 14)

> I feel extremely strongly about this book. It made me very angry too in case an isolated emerging lesbian would read it, and get very upset, despairing, and lonely so I wrote a note in the library book, to tell other readers that women loving women can be beautiful.
>
> (Read in 1982, aged 30)

> Only if they've read other, more positive views of lesbians – too depressing for 'on the turns'.
>
> (Read in 1984, aged 36)

There were often comments that the book should be read in conjunction with other information about lesbians or about that particular period. A number of women said they would only recommend the Virago edition and would advise that the introduction be read first. Many women strongly put the case for the book's historical importance:

Who reads The Well of Loneliness?

> Because of its historical significance in terms of the public image of lesbians – not particularly 'cos of its great literary value!
>
> (Read in 1982, aged 22)

> As an important part of lesbian history and lesbian literary history, yes. I would not recommend it in any sense as a 'slice of lesbian life.'
>
> (Read in 1968, aged 19)

One woman threw an interesting light on why we recommend the book at all. The idea that offering the book to women we suspect may be lesbian as a way of beginning to discuss the whole issue is fairly common, less so is the process she described:

> I recommended it to friends at work at the time – with hindsight as a coming-out gesture; I wouldn't necessarily recommend it to anyone newly coming out – I now know there are more accessible books available.
>
> (Read in 1982, aged 26)

DID THE NOVEL AFFECT LESBIAN IDENTITY?

The concern over the book being read by newly emerging lesbians is linked with the very fragile, and often negative, status of lesbian identity. Internalized shame, guilt, and homophobia are often the worst aspects of lesbian subordination. Women seemed to be making connections between this and reading in their concern that women questioning their sexuality had access to positive images. I was interested, for the same sorts of reasons, in asking women whether they thought reading *The Well of Loneliness* had been useful, harmful, or irrelevant in the development of their lesbian identity. It is not an easy question to answer: thinking deeply about our lives as lesbians has no recognizable shape or significance except, usually, as pathology. More recent developments, particularly around political lesbianism, appear to open that space up a bit more but there is still silence and hesitation. The questionnaire format, too, is impersonal and schematic: a more useful account

Who reads The Well of Loneliness?

could be derived through personal interview, particularly if arranged so that a preliminary discussion could be followed up after time for reflection.

Where women did feel able to comment it was interesting, both for the complexity of reasons given, to explain the usefulness, where it had been and for the depth of feeling attached to those responses where it had been harmful. A significant proportion, 32.5 per cent found it irrelevant, usually because they read the book at a point where their sexual identity was secure. What was fascinating was to find that 14 per cent of women had found the book both useful and harmful: a testimony to the contradictory nature of the text itself and to the sophisticated reading strategies brought to bear upon it:

> It upset me, I didn't want to acknowledge the bad things being lesbian can bring. It could have been harmful, but wasn't. At least it made me come out of dreamland.
>
> (Read in 1982, aged 30)

> Useful in that 'I was not alone' – harmful in that I went through a butch phase, acting a role I didn't really feel; I also thought the outlook seemed grim – went heterosexual for many years until the women's movement made all okay.
>
> (Read in 1965, aged 17)

> Both useful and harmful. I was aware when I read it that it was a classic and had meant a lot to many lesbians for many years. At 13, I was already coming out, so it felt quite significant reading it. At the same time it felt uncomfortable perpetuating the whole lesbian as monster myth.
>
> (Read in 1972, aged 13)

> Useful, but I had to consciously think hard about the homophobic feeling of self-doubt it roused in me. Some of the alienation it describes is part of my own lesbian experience.
>
> (Read in 1984, aged 37)

A smaller percentage than I might have guessed, 7 per cent had found the book harmful. Whether it was chance or not, it seemed that the earlier on in the coming-out process it had been read, and the younger the reader, the more likely it was to produce a strong, negative effect:

Who reads The Well of Loneliness?

The prospect of having to be like Stephen Gordon was terrifying and shaming.

> (Read in 1962, aged 16)

At the time in the 1950s I couldn't identify with the short-back-and-sides, male-suited identity of being a lesbian. Although I was having my first lesbian affair, I felt I wasn't a lesbian.

> (Read in 1953, aged 27)

I was so isolated and inexperienced: I didn't know lesbians, I was too romantic and melodramatic myself, and after *The Well* I thought that lesbian affairs had to end unhappily. And all those bits about the 'damned' race – I was a Catholic.

> (Read in 1979, aged 19)

This left those who had found it useful as the highest proportion, 46.5 per cent in all. The ways in which it was useful varied enormously. For a lot of women, it made them aware of negativity previously not apparent, whether internalized as self-hatred, or external as opinion and attitude.

I had no idea of negative attitudes lesbians might have about themselves – until I met my lover of the time who was an 80s version of Stephen Gordon. The Well was a biography of my lover (who was 21!!) and sadly it helped me to understand her confusion.

> (Read in 1981, aged 33)

The difficulties I faced in becoming a political lesbian are very different from the problem faced by lesbians during the early twentieth century or even 'real' lesbians who are coming out now without the feminist background/context. It helped me to explore the relevance/meaning of butch/femme relationships, and face up to the kind of self-hatred most lesbians lived with and live with on a daily basis. It made me angry at the kind of negation we all have to live with.

> (Read in 1980, aged 18)

I think it touched a deep chord of understanding of the anguish of society's unfairness to lesbian women. It hurt, and I understood and identified with that hurt.

> (Not said when read)

Many women saw it as important simply by existing:

Who reads The Well of Loneliness?

> Useful not so much in terms of developing an identity as in terms of *any* representations of lesbians; in that sense it was a validation.
>
> (Read in 1982, aged 27)

The value of the historical perspective was also picked up by various respondents and used quite differently:

> It was important to me concerning the history of lesbianism. I see it within the time it was written. Although I don't agree with her view of valuing male characteristics and male identity, I take into consideration that in her time the only possible role play within a relationship was a heterosexual one, and that this male/female identity of a couple was the only way she could imagine it.
>
> (Read in 1986, aged 22)

> Useful – gave me a sense of continuity with the past, a historical perspective, a sense of what older lesbians, in particular, must have gone through – the oppression they faced.
>
> (Read in 1981, aged 25)

IDENTIFICATION WITH STEPHEN GORDON

My survey was designed partly to start mapping the reading history of the novel generally, but more specifically to see how significant the character of Stephen Gordon was to lesbian readers. I wanted to elucidate whether the main point of the novel had been her character, whether women admired her or not, and if they identified with her. I found that slightly more women found the novel's focus something other than the character of Stephen Gordon: 53 per cent, which still left a significant number, 47 per cent, for whom she was the point of the novel.

Each response to the question of identification was qualified in some way and it is interesting to see what is taken and what is left. In some cases women identified with Stephen Gordon but found the focus of the novel elsewhere, often in other characters.

I was particularly interested in finding out whether readers had identified with Stephen Gordon and if so what form that

Who reads The Well of Loneliness?

had taken. I was also keen to see whether she was admired and sympathized with, which many readers who did not identify with her did in fact do: 67 per cent of respondents as opposed to 47 per cent who said that they had identified with her. I also wanted to know whether her fortunes had been their main interest in reading the novel.

The answers received to this section of the questionnaire were again testimony to the complexity that reading represents. For instance, although 47 per cent said that the character of Stephen Gordon was the most significant part of the novel for them, they were in the main different women to the 47 per cent who had claimed to identify with Stephen Gordon. The question of identification is one that involves all sorts of theoretical issues about the nature of reading, the formation of subjectivity, and the access we have to that. It is not my intention to address those issues at all. I am drawing on a common-sense use of language as a way of describing a common-sense experience: that of finding empathy and significance in the correspondences between fictional characters and aspects of our own lives. However unreliable such assumptions might be, they are nevertheless recognizable and common amongst readers. Debates about positive images and the promotion of the role models also tie up with this theory of reading: the call for positive representations implies that readers read for identification and are influenced by the nature of the characters they read about.

Of the readers who didn't identify with the character of Stephen Gordon, most were quite clear about what it was in her character that they were rejecting:

> No. Not at all: I have never felt a 'freak', and have never felt God was against me.
>
> > (Read in 1974, aged 25)

> I don't think there is something fundamentally 'wrong' with me, though you cannot help but notice that social pressure dictates otherwise. It has been a while since I read the book, am trying to remember something other than despair about Stephen, I can't. I won't identify with that.
>
> > (Read in 1986, aged 22)

Who reads The Well of Loneliness?

An interesting response that is linked with not identifying with the character of Stephen Gordon, is to see her as in some way a definer of what it is to be a lesbian: 'If anything she made me feel less of a real lesbian. I knew I didn't fit in to the straight world but I knew I didn't fit into Stephen Gordon's either!' (read in 1980, aged 18).

A few readers who read the novel and identified with the character of Stephen Gordon did so for reasons that were nothing to do with lesbianism: 'I had a rural upbringing ... many of her descriptions of freedom in childhood and pain when confronted with social situations rang true. My lesbian relationship, however, is not similar' (read in 1982, aged 40).

The women who identified with Stephen Gordon almost always set out the precise points at which they felt that identification had its power for them. This built up a commentary that differentiated those women who found the most important parts in the pain she represents from those who found in her their only model of lesbianism from those who found her a representative of lesbian struggle.

Proportionally more women found their points of identification with her suffering:

> The difficulties one encounters being a lesbian.
>
> > (Read in 1955, aged 26)

> Yes, unwillingly. I was a lesbian; so was she. That's how I would have to be as an adult.
>
> > (Read in 1962, aged 16)

> Yes: the self-doubt and anguish and the inevitability of sacrificing happiness.
>
> > (Read in 1972, aged 25)

> Yes: her marginality and weirdness.
>
> > (Read in 1972, aged 13)

> Her insecurities and feelings of rejection.
>
> > (Read in 1971, aged 18)

> I identified with S.G.'s anguish – my reservations were/are about having to be so butch!
>
> > (Read in 1953, aged 27)

Who reads The Well of Loneliness?

Yes, there were not many other lesbian characters to identify with.

(Read in 1967, aged 19)

A good number of women stated that although they identified with Stephen Gordon as a lesbian, they were not prepared to see that as involving the identification with the male standards and codes of behaviour that Stephen herself subscribes to:

Yes, in so far as I identified myself as a lesbian but not as that tortured 'pseudo-male' she was portrayed as.

(Read in 1965, aged 20)

Hated her identification with men (the male style, clothes, etc.) but admired her single mindedness and her 'nobility' in doing what she saw as her duty.

(Read in 1984, aged 37)

Yes – I was never into femininity – yes – because I do not want to have relationships with men – yes because I'm oppressed for it sexually. *But* I do not want to be a man!

(Read in 1987, aged 20)

She was too masculine but I did identify with her passion and her love of women.

(Read in 1979, aged 19)

Only in the sense that she was the only 'real lesbian' in the book. I couldn't much identify with the very masculine personna.

(Read in 1982, aged 26)

There was only one woman who saw this as the source of her strength and power as a role model: 'She's quite definitely *a lesbian* unlike more modern heroines. It's very important to her, she takes its implications seriously' (read in 1980, aged 24).

IS STEPHEN GORDON MOST IMPORTANT IN THE NOVEL?

Given such a strong set of reactions to the character of Stephen Gordon, it isn't surprising that such a large number of readers found her character the most significant aspect of the novel. A

Who reads The Well of Loneliness?

good few women found the character of Radclyffe Hall herself more important:

> Yes, in some ways – though even more so it was Radclyffe Hall, for a bit earlier I'd read Una Troubridge's biography of 'John'.
> (Read in 1967, aged 20)

> No, the author's quite understandable self-pity was.
> (Read in 1975, aged 20)

> The bravery of Radclyffe Hall's attempt cannot be overlooked.
> (Read in 1982, aged 40)

A number of women found other characters in the book, especially Puddle, far more significant. A lot of women wrote quite harshly about Mary, but not all:

> I identified more with her partner, especially as I'm a working-class woman from a rather uncaring family who sought to get some nurturing from an older, more successful woman. I saw some parallels between our relationship and the one described in *The Well*.
> (Read in 1984, aged 37)

> Stephen Gordon was so very central that she had to be the most significant character; however, I identified more with Mary.
> (Read in 1982, aged 26)

> Stephen Gordon's the most irritating character in the novel as far as I'm concerned – but other characters, such as Puddle, interest me more.
> (Read in 1968, aged 19)

And some women found the general sketches of lesbian lives more interesting:

> No, the characters in the salons of Paris are the best bit for me.
> (Read in 1987, aged 25)

> No. As a history of that period, the First World War and the women's work in it; the salons in Paris; the book was far more significant.
> (Read in 1971, aged 18)

Who reads The Well of Loneliness?

Many women recognized her centrality, some finding the question puzzling:

> She absorbs all the other characters in the book and is formed by her environment.
>
> > (Read in 1986, aged 22)

> Well, there's not much else, unless you're into horses.
>
> > (Read in 1980, aged 24)

> Was there another part? It portrays an attractive and exciting woman ... most lesbians nowadays chuckle whenever this book is mentioned.
>
> > (Read in 1971, aged 22)

And one woman confessed: 'Yes, I suppose I had a crush on her' (read in 1979, aged 19).

For many women, the importance of Stephen Gordon was less in her specific character than as a representative lesbian:

> Yes, her character as the subject of contempt, fear, hatred, etc., her as an immensely sad and despairing woman.
>
> > (Read in 1986, aged 22)

> I think it was Stephen's character that gave the book its impact – not because she was masculine; but because she was innocent, guileless, honest. She wasn't devious, as lesbians are supposed to be by nature. That may be why I believed in the book in spite of my own better judgement and why it has survived.
>
> > (Read in 1965, aged 17)

This connects with an interest in the book as a document of lesbian history and its significance within lesbian politics.

> No, the fact that the book existed, and had been fought for and was part of our history was the most significant.
>
> > (Read in 1967, aged 19)

> No, the lesbian theme was.
>
> > (Read in 1981, aged 24)

> It was the fact of lesbians being written about and their relationships being valid that was important, but I hated (and still hate) the ending.
>
> > (Read in 1965, aged 20)

Who reads The Well of Loneliness?

I suppose I abstracted the sexual romance and the urgent plea for tolerance from it. I wrote in my diary at the time – or two years after perhaps? – about democracy and the rights of minorities. So it was a political book for me as well as erotic.

(Read in 1964, aged 14)

The understanding it gives of lesbian politics at the time. I respect immensely her courage in writing it.

(Read in 1974, aged 25)

I think her attempts to reach self-acceptance are very moving. I didn't believe then, nor now, that lesbians are 'men in women's bodies' – though some have confusion about identity when coming out as adolescents and getting abuse from families, society, etc. The novel was read primarily as a psychological novel about sexuality, identity, creativity.

(Read in 1981, aged 33)

The silence and protection/destruction of silence.

(Read in 1984, aged 33)

The negative sides to the book are just as interesting – why the need to be so male-dominated – the relinquishing of Mary for a safe heterosexual relationship? Should it be seen as the first 'invert' novel rather than lesbian? Should we describe it as a lesbian novel at all?

(Read in 1987, aged 20)

IS IT AN ACCURATE PICTURE OF LESBIAN LIFE?

This concern with the image of lesbians and lesbianism the novel portrays links with the final set of questions I was asking readers to consider: did the book give an accurate picture of lesbian life and whether or not this mattered. Of the 47 per cent who said that it did, most made it clear that it was a historical view and that things had changed. The 57 per cent who thought the picture of lesbian life it gave did matter were quite clear about why and there was a strong feeling expressed about the dangers of this book being taken as the only version of lesbian existence possible. There were perceptive comments about the impossibility of any one book representing the diversity of experience that makes up 'lesbian life'; at the same time, there

Who reads The Well of Loneliness?

was an understanding that, as a minority experience, any representation would be taken as typical or universal for that minority.

Some women commented that the book did not claim to be realistic and this was important in assessing it:

> I don't think it is a realistic novel in the sense that it attempts to convey day-to-day reality.
>
> (Read in 1968, aged 19)

> What is an 'accurate picture?' I thought it completely possible that lesbians such as Radclyffe Hall could write and think as in *The Well*. I had living experience of the psychological traumas experienced in *The Well*.
>
> (Read in 1981, aged 33)

> Many lesbians at the time apparently felt it was inaccurate and misleading. I don't think it was intended to be *accurate* – rather to persuade people that lesbians were human beings too.
>
> (Read in 1974, aged 25)

Many women found it too stereotyped, or found it true only of a particular time:

> Not an accurate picture of present-day life – obviously, – but it can and has been like that.
>
> (Read in 1965, aged 17)

> Probably for the times but certainly not as a blueprint for the future.
>
> (Read in 1987, aged 20)

> Lesbian life is not a single, homogenous thing. It gave a picture of lesbian life at a certain time/class/psychological moment.
>
> (Read in 1967, aged 19)

> Hall suggests that real lesbians are 1) upper class 2) literary, and 3) have a clique of their own. As a fantasy, this is alright, but it suggests that we're really very rare and also that there's a sort of lesbian promised land out there, which is depressing and untrue.
>
> (Read in 1965, aged 17)

> I was 16 and assumed the portrayal of these adult lesbians must be accurate.
>
> (Read in 1962, aged 16)

Who reads The Well of Loneliness?

> Obviously it was sentimentalized and playing up to straight fantasies about lesbians, but I think we've internalized those images as well to the extent that that's what some lesbians become. So in a kind of negative, twisted way it was accurate.
>
> (Read in 1972, aged 13)

The rather sanguine approach to whether or not it was accurate went once women were considering whether or not the question of accuracy mattered. The woman who spoke about lesbians internalizing those negative images went on:

> Not necessarily, in a context of novels of a more positive focus coming out. But *The Well of Loneliness* unfortunately became so well known *because* of its lurid perspective so I guess in the end the inaccuracies do matter.
>
> (Read in 1972, aged 13)

Some women pointed out again the problem of any one book representing all lesbian experience:

> One can't have an accurate picture of lesbian life; every life is so different.
>
> (Read in 1982, aged 30)

> It would be very difficult to write a book that all lesbians could identify with given class, race, politics, etc.
>
> (Read in 1977, aged 27)

And for women who see the book primarily as a historical document, the issue of inaccuracy is less important:

> No, life changes.
>
> (Read in 1967, aged 19)

> Not if the book is read in context with awareness of how sexologists' views on lesbianism influenced Hall.
>
> (Read in 1981, aged 24)

Women who were concerned about the novel's inaccuracies tended to be concerned about the ways in which this one experience of lesbianism was taken to be the only, or the most authoritative, view:

Who reads The Well of Loneliness?

It matters when it's described as a lesbian novel and so may be taken as an accurate picture of lesbian life.

(Read in 1987, aged 20)

Yes, especially for those people who only have this book as information about what 'being lesbian' is about.

(Read in 1967, aged 20)

Only if people think it is the whole picture.

(Read in 1975, aged 20)

It probably does matter. The kinds of novels we write even now don't often get across the fact that lesbians are everywhere.

(Read in 1965, aged 17)

Yes it does matter if the reader is led to believe the book is 'the' portrait of lesbian life.

(Read in 1986, aged 22)

It matters very greatly: we need positive images.

(Read in 1962, aged 16)

I don't think it makes any difference to its literary merit or lack of it as a novel, but it does have social repercussions for both lesbians and heterosexuals because of the peculiar status of the book as the quintessential lesbian novel.

(Read in 1968, aged 19)

The Well of Loneliness is, whether loved, respected, or hated, one of the most important books within our lesbian culture. Reading these responses to the novel, it becomes clear how important books and reading are to lesbians, often the only public discourse about lesbianism to which there is access. The pressure on authors to produce useful and truthful representations of lesbian life is enormous. As lesbian readers, our skills in reading generally – which are developed through years of reading against the grain of heterosexual culture – take on a new dimension, which is to extract from apparently unpromising texts, lessons of inspiration and encouragement for lesbian lives. Talking to lesbians about their reading histories, this reading for whatever we can get from unpromising, often heterosexual or homophobic writers develops early and is then, sadly, often needed in reading our own lesbian tradition: filling

Who reads The Well of Loneliness?

in its gaps, imagining the positive outcomes we want and need. In asking women to share their experiences of reading *The Well of Loneliness*, I was tapping in to a wealth of knowledge that too often remains hidden in lesbian lives: information we do not get enough opportunity to exchange and build on. Many women went back to their diaries, as did a friend who wrote when I first started work on this book:

> It's dated 25 February 1972, by which time one might have expected a little more maturity. However ... 'I reread (masochistically) *The Well of Loneliness*, and noticed this time the motto: Nothing extenuate, /Nor set down ought in malice. It hurts to read that book and must have hurt so much to write it and yet she does keep to her motto. She has the courage I lack noticeably, and says so much that is true. At the moment I'm living in utmost cowardice – the cowardice of those who do not state what they are – in other words living a lie. It is hard and difficult certainly.... But the happy parts of *The Well of Loneliness* make me very envious and longing, and I'm thrown back on boring (and by now generally unsatisfactory) dreams.' Make of it what you will but keep it hidden.
>
> (Read in 1972, aged 22, reproduced with permission)

CONCLUSION

The overall conclusions indicate less about ways of valuing a writer like Radclyffe Hall or a character like Stephen Gordon, than a clear sense of the need to develop a lesbian criticism, which accounts for different lesbian readers' experience of books and writing. The partial and indirect access that lesbians – and other readers – have to lesbian books and the connections between those books, writers, and readers, makes traditional views of literary history: even alternative traditions such as the feminist criticism developed by such women as Elaine Showalter, irrelevant.

Situated outside of linear historical time, lesbian readers and readings move in and out of the traditions and institutions of literature: the whole idea of development, progressive images, and the questions of literary history, biography, and critical readings are reformulated around the axis of value. Conventional methods of assessing and valuing writing cease to have the same application in a context in which the social and psychological demands are foregrounded: where reading as a lesbian involves a procedure that draws on and is referred back to politics and cultural possibility, as well as to literary judgement.

Literary judgement, especially in the formation of tradition, is a process of retaining and discarding books and authors, relevant and useful ideas and achievements. Whatever general observations can be made about the partiality of the mainstream traditions, it is clear that when considering lesbian

Conclusion

writing, the question of discarding or moving beyond certain books and authors is far from straight forward. There is so little lesbian writing, and access to both the writing and discussion of the subject is so difficult that we all must, and do, take what we can from everything around us. A writer like Radclyffe Hall, who contains such contradictions for lesbians, whether contemporary or not, feminist or not, is a powerful example of this. What we make of her, the centrality of all those qualifications and reservations in the questionnaires, is testimony to the hard work each lesbian does, in her reading and her life, to move beyond oppression.

> after all my protests against
> glorifying our oppression
> . . .
> I realised again that
> our oppression is our culture
> or at least it has been
> for many lesbians up to now
> the role thing and the bar thing defining
> the only territory where we could live out
> the lies that passed for our lives
> instead of the lies
> that passed for someone elses
>
> (from Dyke Jacket by Fran Winant 1973)

BIBLIOGRAPHY

WORKS BY RADCLYFFE HALL

Hall, R. (1908) *A Sheaf of Verses*, London: John and Edward Bumpus.
Hall, R. (1934) *Miss Ogilvy Finds Herself*, London: Heinemann.
Hall, R. (1924) *The Unlit Lamp*, London: Cassells.
Hall, R. (1982) *The Well of Loneliness*, London: Virago.

WORKS ABOUT RADCLYFFE HALL

Baker, M. (1985) *Our Three Selves*, London: Hamish Hamilton.
Brittain, V. (1968) *A Case of Obscenity*, London: Femina.
Dickson, L. (1975) *Radclyffe Hall At The Well of Loneliness: A Sapphic Chronicle*, London and Glasgow: Collins.
Egan, B. (1928) *The Sink of Solitude*, London: Hermes Press.
Franks, C. S. (1982) *Beyond The Well of Loneliness*, Aldershot, Hampshire: Avebury.
Ormrod, R. (1984) *Una Troubridge: The Friend of Radclyffe Hall*, London: Jonathan Cape.
Troubridge, Una, Lady (1961) *The Life and Death of Radclyffe Hall*, London: Hammond and Hammond.

ARTICLES

McNaron, T. A. H. (1982) 'A journey into otherness: teaching *The Well of Loneliness*', in M. Cruikshank (ed.) *Lesbian Studies Present and Future*, New York: The Feminist Press.
Newton, E. (1985) 'The mythic mannish lesbian: Radclyffe Hall and

Bibliography

the new woman', in Freedman; E. B. et al (ed.) *The Lesbian Issue: Essays from Signs*, Chicago: University of Chicago Press.

Radford, J. (1986) 'An Inverted Romance: *The Well of Loneliness* and sexual ideology', in *The Progress of Romance*, London: Routledge.

Ruehl, S. (1982) 'Inverts and Experts: Radclyffe Hall and the lesbian identity', in R. Brunt and R. Coward (eds.) *Feminism, Culture and Politics*, London: Lawrence & Wishart.

OTHER WORKS CONSULTED

Barnes, D. (1928) *The Ladies Almanack*, Dijon: Darantierre.

Benson, E. F. (1985) *As We Were*, London: Hogarth.

Ellis, H. (1924); *Studies in the Psychology of Sex*, London and Watford: University of London Press.

Faderman, L. (1981) *Surpassing The Love of Men*, London: The Women's Press.

von Krafft-Ebbing; R. (1892) *Psychopathia Sexualis*, London: F. J. Rebman.

Moers, E. (1977) *Literary Women*, London: W.H. Allen.

Roberts, J.R. (1979) 'In America they call us dykes', *Sinister Wisdom* 9, Spring 1979.

Rich, A. (1979) *Some Notes on Honour and Lying*, London: Onlywomen Press.

Rule, J. (1975) *Lesbian Images*, Trumansburg, N.Y.: The Crossing Press.

Showalter, E. (1978) *A Literature of Their Own*, London: Virago.

Smith, H. Z. (1931) *Not So Quiet ... Step-daughters of War*, London: George Newnes.

Winant, F. (1973) 'Dyke Jacket' in E. Bulkin and J. Larkin *Lesbian Poetry*, Massachusetts: Persephone.